Eagle's Mead

Vinndu af verkum inn verðuga mjöð!

Eagle's Mead

Initiatory Poetry and Prose

Eirik Westcoat

Skaldic Eagle Press
Long Branch, Pennsylvania
2019

For permissions or other information, please contact
the author at <eirik@theskaldiceagle.com>
or <www.theskaldiceagle.com>.

Cover art by David Rudziński
All layout, typesetting, and interior art by Eirik Westcoat

First Edition, Ostara 2019

9 8 7 6 5 4 3 2 1

Casewrap Hardcover ISBN: 978-1-947407-06-0

Skaldic Eagle Press
Long Branch, Pennsylvania

For the Rune-Gild

Acknowledgements

First and foremost, my thanks go the Rune-Gild, to which this book is dedicated and without which this book would not exist. My Quests for the Mead, Runes, and Grails started with them, and my work of self-transformation in that august initiatory school is what produced the majority of the content in this book. There is much poetry here that is directly inspired by and written about its rites and curriculum, and the source of any given poem will often not be obvious or mentioned.

Next, my thanks go to two particular individuals in the Rune-Gild. First is Edred, its founder, who created the inspiring rites and curriculum just mentioned and without whom the Rune-Gild would not have come into being. Second is ᚱᛁᚺᛏᛏᛁ, who was my mentor and guide on the road to Mastery — his personal example and way of being are an inspiration to all who know him.

Outside of the Rune-Gild, I have two other initiates to thank. First is ᚠᚠᚾᛁᛏᚾᛁ, who has shown a path of upward striving and inspiration. Second is ᚷᛦᛏᚾᚠᚱᛁ, who has helped me tend the flame of that which was lost.

Special thanks go to the following for their particular roles in getting this book ready for publication:
• For his fierce and striking cover art: David Rudziński.
• For copyediting and corrections: Alice Karlsdóttir and P.D. Brown.
• For final proofing of the print-ready file: Scott Shell.

Thanks also go to the many unnamed people who have seen or heard various poems in this collection prior to publication and have given me feedback or praise for them.

Finally, thanks go to the wise one himself, Óðinn, the great Germanic exemplar of self-transformation. His example is at the root of much of the above, and it is he who is the eternal Drighten of the Mead, Runes, and Grails.

Table of Contents

The Good of Galdralag: An Inspired Look
into Modern Uses for the Meter.

Runes for the Grails:
Creating Old English Rune Poem Stanzas
for Cweorð, Calc, Stān, and Gār.

Whom Does (the Story of) the Grail Serve?
The Chivalric Ideals Communicated in Chrétien's Romances.

Afterword

Foreword

Invocation

On main of Mead I've fed
to move higher and prove
Spirit's spark in my core:
spurred to fly like a bird.
I pour its potent fire
for people need indeed
rebirth to bring now forth
the boons of Óðinn's runes.

Preface

This is a book for initiates, magicians, occultists, esotericists, sages, heathen prophets, and other travelers of the hidden realms, one that will not be understood by others. What you are about to read is the record of a journey, one that I hope will offer you inspiration and signposts for your own journey. Specifically, it is my journey of esoteric initiatory work up to this point, primarily through the Rune-Gild and its curriculum, *The Nine Doors of Midgard* — although it went beyond these also. (If you have read or, better yet, worked through *The Nine Doors of Midgard*, you'll get much more out of this book than those who have not.) In that way, my initiatory work started with the Runes, but it very quickly came to encompass the Mead as well. Together, these two would later lead me to the Grails. This great triad of quests — for the Mead, the Runes, and the Grails — has come to define my personal initiatory path and will likely continue to do so for the rest of my life. Nearly all of the pieces in this book were written from 2011–2017 (from the earliest stages of my initiatory journey in the Rune-Gild through shortly after my Naming as a Rune-Master in it), and all relate quite directly to one or more of those three quests.

In the Rune-Gild, one must demonstrate one's developing level of being by producing tangible works. The first such advancement, from Learner to Fellow, requires the production of a short piece known as a Fellowship Work. The second such advancement, from Fellow to Master, requires the production of a much more substantial piece known as a Master Work. This book is not my official Rune-Gild Master Work, but it is fair to say that it may represent a second, unofficial one. It is, top to bottom, a demonstration of the power of traditional poetry for initiatory work. It is, at its heart, the work of developing my wode-self, one of the core aspects of Rune-Gild training. It is also something that shows I have used the Runic tradition as a tool of my Ascent and gained extensive knowledge of its idiom, lore, and techniques — while covering the main tenets of this Work in a poetic fashion.

There are charms, spells, and ritual workings in this book, and some cautionary words on them are in order. Most were written before I had a high-enough level of being to make good use of them. I am surely not quite as impressive as this book might make me appear. In many ways, it serves as the distant star that guides me to the Self ahead of myself that I am striving to reach. So it is my task to truly apply the things in this book. The results of the reader who attempts to use these incantations will vary based on his or her own level of Initiation and Understanding of what is written here. The wise reader, however, will know where to make modifications to adapt these formulas for his or her own unique journey.

As that implies, it is likely that there are things in here that are of subjective value only to myself. But the overall method of the use of traditional Germanic poetry for esoteric work is one that does have objective, transpersonal value and utility. It is still not for all, however. For many, it will not be their cup of tea. But for a few, it may well be an exhilarating draught of the Mead. Yet I hope all who read it will come to appreciate the beauty of traditional Germanic poetry, regardless of their level of initiation — as all of the poetry is written in modern English versions of traditional alliterative meters. (Short descriptions of these meters may be found in my book of religious poetry, *Viking Poetry for Heathen Rites*.)

Some remarks on the chapters will help orient the reader:

- "Opening" sets the tone of this book and gives rightful due to Óðinn, the great Germanic exemplar of self-transformation. It also features my poem about being a poet, which is central to my Work.
- "Wode and Fetch" represents the highest aspects and strivings of my Self, and how the three quests relate to my magical personas. This collection is part personal mission statement and part magical utterance combined in a mythopoetic medium. More here than elsewhere, the reader will notice names given in runes instead of profane letters. These are almost always in the old languages, either Old Norse, Proto-Germanic, or Old English, using the Younger Fuþark, Elder Fuþark, or Anglo-Saxon Fuþorc, respectively. Any decent guide to runic transliteration will facilitate a rough pronunciation, but more will not be supplied here.
- "The Work of Nine Doors" is my poetic summary and commentary on the complete public curriculum of the Rune-Gild. For me, finishing this collection in late 2013 was necessary for me to truly mark my completion of the Doors and integrate the fruits of them into my being, so that I could then more properly move on to other things. *The Nine Doors of Midgard* probably appears bewildering to most the first time they read it, and I was certainly no exception. It is my hope that those reading these poems will thus gain a better grasp on just what the work entails and what they can get out of it.
- "Sjálfsljóðin" is one of the products of my Personal Analysis Diary work of relating the rune staves to aspects of my life that required strengthening or transforming. It is one example of combining poetry and runes for magical work. I finished it in late 2011.
- "Runecraft: A New Rúnatal" is modeled after *Hávamál* 138–45 in many regards. I wrote this in mid-2014 as an unofficial Fellowship Work relating directly to the Runes. At 729 lines, it was also my

first attempt at a very long poem in the style of continuous verse found in Anglo-Saxon poetry.

- "The Ascent of a Grail Knight" was completed in late 2016. It was my means of orienting myself in the Grail mysteries within an initiatory framework. It helped me to understand the nature of my initiatory journey so far, and it revealed to me some pieces of how my journey might go in the future towards higher and more perilous levels. It is also my longest narrative poem to date at 983 lines.

- "Initiatory Sumbel Toasts" starts a series of chapters of shorter poems. This chapter represents my use of sumbel toasts as magical utterances for self-development. Most readers would not attempt to use them verbatim for their own workings, but I think all rune magicians could find value in them as a model for how to enhance the magical power of a traditional heathen sumbel.

- "Mead-Work Poems" relate to my Mead quest. All are about direct work with the Mead, yet in very different ways.

- "Rune-Work Poems" are my various Rune Poems, whether loose translations or originals. The three "Working" poems are about certain Rune-Work rituals.

- "Grail-Work Poems" are short poetic pieces bringing a Germanic heathen flavor to the Grail Mythos. The Grail Slam pieces in particular were an important foray into connecting my heathen vision into the more established Grail traditions. They are called the Grail Slam because they were designed as a sequence of poems that might be entered into a poetry slam. "Ask the Question" is a cryptic personal piece on integrating that particular theme of the earliest Grail romances into my life.

- "Charms and Invocations" are all short pieces that rune magicians may find use for. Several are inspired by elements in *The Nine Doors of Midgard*. The "Staves for the Self" at the end of the chapter is another piece derived from my Personal Analysis Diary Work. Its structure is modeled on that part of *Hávamál* called the "Ljóðatal."

- "Workings and Blessings" are powerful rites for bringing the Mead, the Runes, and the Grails into one's life. Perhaps they are too powerful to be in here. Of course, a certain level of runic initiation is necessary to access the full power of these rites.
- "The Good of *Galdralag*" is the revised version of part two of my official Fellowship Work in the Rune-Gild, dealing with one particular aspect of the Mead: the possible uses of the *galdralag* meter in modern poetry. It was originally written in September 2012. It represents the practical and inspired application of part one of my Fellowship Work, which is my scholarly research into the *galdralag* meter that was published in the Viking Society's *Saga-Book* 40 (2016).
- "Runes for the Grails" describes my process of innovating an extension to the Old English Rune Poem. For me, it formed an unofficial Fellowship Work relating to the Grails. It was originally going to be my official Fellowship Work, but before I started writing it, I instead made my *galdralag* material into my Fellowship Work. However, the allure of this idea stayed with me, and I wrote it in late 2013. Its completion had quite a profound effect on me, irrevocably committing me to the Grail Quest. I consider my scholarly publication in the journal *Odroerir*, "The Valknut: Heart of the Slain?", to be a kind of sequel to this, and the interested reader should definitely follow up with it.
- "Whom Does (the Story of) the Grail Serve?" was written in late 2014, originally for a course on the chivalric romances of Chrétien de Troyes. It represents another piece of my development in my Grail Quest, in looking to what those romances say about the ideals of Knighthood.

In producing all of these works, I directly experienced the truth of Óðinn's claim that "A word got a word by a word for me; a work got a work by a work for me." Now deeply drink these words, that they may get you more words.

Eirik Westcoat
Ostara 2019

Opening

A Skaldic Eagle Takes Flight

Hatched from the Egg, he was hungry always;
that cosmic hailstone crafted such wyrd.
In size he surged, consuming carrion:
strong and stately, he stood at last.
He was sleek and fierce, but unsatisfied.
That fleshy fodder had fulfilled its end,
but such food no longer could feed his soul.
His keen cold eyes, they craved new vistas,
and his heart sought out the holy mysteries.
To the Cave he went, that court of darkness
and Lunar land of limitless night,
seeking its treasures for his soul's triumph.
He came at last to cauldrons three
filled with the ferment of fathomless Spirit.
He drank down that Mead and from dreams awoke
to soul's satisfaction and Solar gnosis.
A seed of Self he saw within,
and now at last he knew himself
as the eagle he was. Then up he flew,
to the heights he soared and their healthful freedom;
the sun he sought in Ascent and joy.
With gnosis now of these new vistas,
he poured out poetry in a powerful torrent,
a sparkling stream of Spirit's essence.
He remembered the land and meant to return,
but gray and grim the ground realms seemed;
one tear he shed for that world he'd lost,
though aid he'd offer to the others down there

by decanting Mead to the curious ones
who sought the Sky. Ere soaring again
(above-aiming to the abode of Spirit),
on the taller trees for a time he'd rest,
and among the majesty of the mountain peaks.
Truly this happens, time and again:
the birth and rebirth — a bittersweet tale —
of a Skaldic Eagle in the Sky above.

Initiation and Rebirth

About rebirth
I built these staves —
the greatest work
of gods and men.
I tell a tale
of trial and death,
of life anew
in lifted being.

Here have I hung
in hunger and thirst
upon that tree,
tallest of all.
As Óðinn I died
in awesome ordeal;
through a spell in darkness
my spirit then fared.

Under the world,
I witnessed beginning:
the ash and elm
by Óðinn were gifted

2

with being, breath,
and bright good looks.
Humanity's birth
I made my own.

For wisdom I fared
to worlds all nine;
their timeless patterns
I took as a guide.
On roads between
I realized much;
my spirit soared,
seeking it all.

I lifted the lore
at last in darkness:
the sacra I sought,
the singular Runes!
My spirit returned
to the tree I was at,
embodied anew
on a brighter day.

I'm new in my spirit,
new in my body,
new in my soul,
new in my heart,
and reborn at last
— being initiated —
to work in the world
with wisdom great.

Óðinsdrápa

For the master of mead
I make my praise
— that rowner and rister
of runic might —
and pour his drink
— that precious draught —
in the potent staves
of a powerful drápa.

Borr by Bestla
gave birth to him,
Búri and Bölþorn's
brightest descendant.
The etin Ymir
Óðinn then slew
and ordered the earth
by his own design.

The sun and moon
he set on courses;
each realm he gave
a rightful place.
The worlds were made,
yet he wanted more;
he sensed the unknown
and sought its mystery.

On the Tree he hung
with terrible hunger
nights numbered nine
in needful ordeal;
with a look and scream

he skillfully lifted
gainful knowledge
of the glorious Runes.

Joyous Óðinn
is a generous lord,
for among the worlds
those mysteries he shared.
He bids us follow
and benefit too,
by giving ourselves
and gaining ourselves.

He always seeks
to add to his wisdom,
for awesome Óðinn
is of Aesir best!

The art of Seið
he sought from his mistress;
of might and main,
it's a major source.
He laid with Freyja
and learned its secrets;
by knowing mystery,
magic is gained.

Famous Freyja's
fimbul magic
is another part
of needful questing;
through the depths of trance
in darkness and light,

singular secrets
are sought and found.

He presses onward;
no path is forbidden,
for awesome Óðinn
is of Aesir best!

Mímir gave Hœnir
mighty counsels,
until his head
was hewn from his neck.
But Sigtýr saved
that source of wisdom
by spreading on herbs
and uttering spells.

Of hidden things
the head of Mímir
speaks now to Óðinn,
adding to his knowledge.
The challenge to us,
if we choose to accept,
is to seek for ourselves
this source of knowing.

His many quests
are mighty examples,
for Óðinn always
aims for glory!

In the well he sought
transcendent wisdom;
but Mímir demanded

a mighty price —
Óðinn must offer
an eye to the well.
He paid in full
for that precious drink.

An eye for the tree,
an eye for the well;
in all the realms
he's able to see.
He never asks
of his Einherjar
for more than what
he's managed to do.

The powers he's gained
are great indeed,
for Óðinn always
aims for glory!

But the greatest treasure
he took from Gunnlöð —
the mightiest mead,
made from Kvasir.
Three draughts he got
for three nights' lust;
the sneaky serpent
then soared as eagle.

This best of bounties
he bears to the few
— skalds and scholars —
for skill with words.
To win and pour

that potion as well
is the mighty challenge
he makes to them.

At the end of all,
Óðinn faces
the giant jaws
of the jaundiced wolf.
He is swallowed whole,
and his son avenges,
ripping apart
the ravenous beast.

Transformed he lives
in famed survivors:
in Hœnir made whole
and as Höð and Baldur,
in valiant Víðarr
and Váli his brother;
a mysterious triumph
o'er tragedy and death.

His noble quests
I've named in verse
with this mead I made
and mixed with runes;
drink it deeply
and dare to follow
in mighty Óðinn's
mainful footsteps!

Wode and Fetch

Wode-Tally

The Quests I keep
quicken my Self;
in these three I thrive and grow:
seeking the Mead,
seeking the Runes,
and seeking the glorious Grails.

These greatest Works
are guided by Words
in the realm that's right to each:
in the Well, *Óðrœrir*,
on the Wood, *Rûna*,
and to soar for the Sun, *Upstiġe*.

Precious Wode
and potent Wisdom
are blended with brightest Wynn,
as I become
all in my questing
that comes from the core of my being.

My Lady gives life
and light to these works;
it all is hallowed to her.
She is ᚠᚪᚦᛞᚱᛁᚠᛗ
and shining ᛏᛚᚪᚱᚾᛏ
and magic ᛗᛋᛞᚾᛈᚪᛏ united.

Tried and tested,
I triumphed well,
and gained the goals I sought.
I drank from Cup,
I deemed with Gar,
and I lived by steadfast Stone.

As mighty *Skáld*
and mainful *Erilaz*
and boldly thundering *Þegn*,
my Work continues
in the Worlds and the Gilds
as I dare for life 'yond death.

I am ᚠᚨᚦᛒᚨᚱᚠ
and ᚹᚨᚱᛗᛒᚨᚾᚠ
and wondrous ᚹᚢᛏᛗᚨᚱᛏᚱᚾ;
I am ᚠᛏᚠᚠᚱᚢᚦᛁ
and ᚷᚨᛁᛃᚠᚠᚠᚢᛗᛁᚤ
and gallant ᚼᚱᚠᛏᚠᚦᛗᚷᚾ;
they all are merged in me.

ᚠᚨᚦᛒᚨᚱᚠ, *Raiser of Spirit*

I, ᚠᚨᚦᛒᚨᚱᚠ, from the Well within,
won the great goal of glorious Wode.
With serpent facade I sought *Óðrœrir*
and its grandest Cup, a crafty Grail.
Under Tree's roots I angled and turned,
piercing the mountain then piercing that maiden,
like Óðinn with Gunnlöð in the honored tales.
Welded with ᚠᚨᚦᛗᚱᛁᚠᛗ, I waxed in greatness:
draughts three I drank, deed-thirsty ever.

Then fury-filled, I forcefully acted,
burning that fuel on a bonfire of Self
to send my soul soaring to new heights.
With great gifts gained, I grew and throve.
Prophecy's power pours from my lips:
I speak with main my spells of fortune.
Fierce flaming fire comes forth from my mouth:
with runes on my tongue, I write with my voice.
Verse I've mastered in various meters,
the sonic substance that surges with Mead.
With Ale, Ayahuasca, and Absinthe I've waxed,
loosing the spirits that speed within them.
I bear the serpent as my sign and boon
of the might and main that I've mastered thus.
With the awesome Cup, I offer those gifts
with the frenzied spirit that speeds the Folk,
that madness-fomenter. The main-filled blood,
the lunar force, and the living Waters:
Cup's craft they carry, and they call to my Wode.
To the realm of gods, I then raise my being,
and stain my runes with that strongest substance:
from the darkest depths I draw pure light.

ᚹᚪᚱᛗᛒᚫᚾᛞ, *Warrior of Woden*

I, ᚹᚪᚱᛗᛒᚫᚾᛞ, from the Wood within,
won the great goal of glorious Wisdom.
Always ᛏᚠᚢᚱᚾᛏ has urged me to seek,
so as horse I galloped through the heart of each world
to gain the Runes and a Grail that's noble,
the Gar of sovereignty. I sought *Rûna*
and faced my death, transfixed on the Tree,
and gave to my Self a gift of self.

11

Transformed I fell, with fimbul gains,
and reordered my self for reordering the world,
by risting the runes with right discipline
and my noble will. With nine glory-twigs,
I slew the serpents that sucked at my tree.
Their hearts' blood I drank, like the hero Sigurd
to gain their powers for my glorious deeds:
I wield their darkness as a weapon of daring.
I read my runes to righteously know
the boons of wyrd's work. Of above and below,
I worked a synthesis in my well of soul
so that I draw Wisdom from the deepest roots
and the highest branches of my holy tree.
For Mímir's drink I made a sacrifice:
to inner territories, I turned an eye.
As a Warrior of Woden, in the world I act.
I work in wood the wyrd I choose;
with daily deemings I deal my will.
Like Kvasir I share, my craft I transmit;
I teach what I am for the triumph of others.
I emulate Óðinn with the awesome Gar:
that brand of fire is blood-summoning,
with the prime power of the polar force.
By seeking mysteries to Seek the Mystery,
bright light and bleak dark I've blended inside.

ᛈᛚᛏᛗᚨᚱᛏᚱᚻ, *Solar Seeker*

I, ᛈᛚᛏᛗᚨᚱᛏᚱᚻ, awake to the Sun,
won the great goal of glorious Wynn.
Ever onward, in this endless quest,
I sought *Upstige* and soared as an eagle
— from the draught I drank of the dearest Mead —

to gain the Grails and the glorious Stone.
With strength through joy I journey the strait-road
to the castle keep that's called Montsalvat,
seeking transcendence to see the world
with true vision and timeless wisdom,
as a fiery spirit freed from the Waters.
A glimpse of that realm, a gift from Self
of spiritual gnosis, spurred me to action.
My Grail Maiden, great ᛗᛇᛞᚢᚹᚣᚾ,
shewed me the Stone that shines in my core
with the overflowing, fullest happiness;
it quickened my work. Through querth's turning,
I conquered the grave with crafty Fire:
from my own ashes, I rose up to life,
with right consecration as a runic aristocrat
of the Soul and Self. I seek Tradition
through valued traditions in a revolt against
the mundane world. With Mead and Runes
I presence Spirit as a potent example
of the solar force that flows from the Center.
By Royal Art, I ride the tiger
in this crapped-up world of the Kali Yuga:
though the world may wane, I wax stronger.
My heart is bold, heavy with compassion,
yet steady as stone. I strive for the mountains,
for the grandest peaks. On such glorious wings,
I'm carried aloft; I become the light.

ᚴᚾᛚᚠᚱᚢᚦᛁ, *Skald of Óðrœrir*

I, ᚴᚾᛚᚠᚱᚢᚦᛁ,
as a Gild sibling,
have written runes with gar!

My Quest is the Mead
that quickens the soul
and fills it with poetry's power.

Wise in *gal-*,
I waxed in greatness
through work as skald and scholar.
In pouring poems
and pondering lore,
I gained through galdralag.

Marked with name
by Master ᚱᛁᚼᛏᛏᛁ,
I rose in rank in the Gild.
By gand of cherry,
my growth was honored
and my name was firmly fastened,
and my doom was firmly forged.

Óðrœrir I sought,
the awesome mead,
for fimbul words and works!
I worked some bale
to win that boon,
but here I'll name it not.

As snake I sneaked,
seeking Hnitbjörg
and the maiden of mead within.
Filled with virility,
I filled that woman
and united our natures twain.

With the mead I drank,
my main increased
and I soared as awesome eagle.
Asgard I reached,
the Aesir's realm,
as a poet of greater potency,
as a poet ascending in soul.

Pouring out
the precious mead
is also my awesome charge.
By Rûna's power
and runes on my tongue,
my words are filled with wode!

I work now magic
with wode-stirring mead,
but I'm ever seeking onward,
for many are the forms
of mighty Óðrœrir
that the wise must win and pour.

As Skald of Óðrœrir,
my skills are waxing
in thoughts and words and works.
With mead I've made
a Master Work
to honor both Gaut and Gild,
to honor both Self and Soul!

ᚷᚨᛁᛉᚨᚹᚨᛚᛞᚨᛉ, Weaver of Wyrd

I, ᚷᚨᛁᛉᚨᚹᚨᛚᛞᚨᛉ, with great perseverance,
sought the mysteries and sovereignty's might
as Woden did in the world's beginning.

I would wield my gar; thus wounded by gar
I gave a gift on the glorious ash
of myself to Self through sacred work.

I drank my death in a draught from a vine,
then at last I looked below its roots;
raging fiercely, Rûna I grasped.

I found the runes and the fimbul songs;
I drank from a grail the dearest mead;
In wisdom's work I waxed and throve.

The worlds I sought and won their secrets;
the skills I gained to score my triumphs;
by quest I was tested; I quickened greatly.

A serpent I slew: it sailed in the sky
and wound its way on windy streams;
I sipped from that snake its sanguine essence.

A storm had crashed: I strove quickly,
acting with all to end the crisis;
through hail I hallowed my higher Self.

I grove the runes with reddened gar,
reweaving my wyrd with wondrous staves;
my sovereign Self soared to new heights.

With runes as seeds in the root of my soul,
I'm well prepared for the work ahead
as I will to cross the wide abyss.

ᚷᚱᚪᛚᛚᚦᛖᚷᚾ, *Knight of the Grails*

I, ᚷᚱᚪᛚᛚᚦᛖᚷᚾ, a gallant knight,
took up the Quest to quicken my spirit:
to seek and gain for my soul the Grails!
Like knights of old, I needed virtues:
acting with Honor to all who merit,
dogged Faithfulness to Tradition and Quest,
and Chivalry to guide my shining life.
As a Page I prepared with purest deeds.
The Oak I nurtured, for noble troth.
The Ash I became, to own my stead.
The Bow I strung, for the battle ahead.
I knew not the goal, yet galloped onward;
rightly I rode, though I realized not.
In Runes and Mead, I remembered myself,
and glimpsed the glory of the Grail mysteries;
my Work found Purpose and waxed in might.
As a Squire I endured the squalls within.
The Serpent I became for switching worlds.
The Grave I faced, that grim ending.
The Querth I turned and quickened my fire.
On the poet's path, I proudly rode,
seeking the essence of the awesome Grails.
An Ascent I seized for my substance within:
I wrought in my soul the righteous virtues
of wynn, permanence, and wise nobility,
and fulfillment found this phase of my Quest.
As Knight of the Grails, I name my gains.

The Cup I drank, that keenest draught.
The Stone I became, steadfast in my core.
The Gar I wielded for the greatest works.
The Grails I gained, those glorious mysteries!
My being is bound to that bright triad,
and to a great beyond, a gate they've opened.

Wode-Selves Drápa

I, ᚠᚨᚦᛒᚨᚱᛋ,
awake at last,
rise to glory
and greatness now!
As ᛈᚢᚱᛗᛒᚨᚾᛋ
I wax in might;
as ᛈᚢᛚᛗᚨᚱᛏᚱᛁ
my wode I pour.

To secure my rise
I carved my runes
in a stave of oak
and stained them red;
my being is boosted
by a band of silver,
the awesome ring
that's ᛏᛚᚢᚠᚠᛗ hight.

I always follow
the Odian path,
with thoughts and words
and thunderous works.
Sovereign virtues
I seek to live

through hugh and myne
and hallowed wode.

The main of my work
is mighty wode:
with will it's summoned
and wyrd it alters.
For magic I make
the mead inside;
I speak and write
with this spirited flow.

With boldness bright
and brimming courage,
I fearlessly act
— confronting the world —
asserting myself
to seek my goals,
clearly confident
and with craft of wode.

Awesome Óðrœrir
I earnestly seek.
Wonders I work
as Wode-Bearer.

As scholar I work
with skillful craft:
the books I write
are a boon to my field.
I excel in service,
research and teaching
as a famed professor
from the Folk of Woden.

As skald I work
with skillful craft:
the poems I pour
are potent draughts.
In masterful meter
I make my verse;
it stirs the wode
of Woden's Folk.

I rown the Runes
that I rightly seek.
Wonders I work
as Wode-Bearer.

The work of the Gild
I well perform
to hang on the Tree
for its hallowed treasure.
Like Óðinn before,
I've earned the Runes
by giving myself
for gain to Self.

The might and main
of mysteries I won;
those steadfast staves
I stained in my soul.
By these brightest boons,
my being was changed
and lifted up
to lofty heights.

To gain in soul,
the Grails I seek.

Wode with wisdom
and wynn I pour.

In Quest as a Knight,
quickening I sought
through the greatest glory
of gods and men:
the Holy Grails
of highest renown;
with Mead and Runes,
I made my way.

The Cup I drank,
that keenest draught.
The Gar I wielded
for the greatest works.
The Stone I became,
steadfast in my core.
The Grails I gained,
those glorious mysteries!

A fimbul fire
fueled my rising!
Wode with wisdom
and wynn I pour.

Radiant charisma
and unrelenting youth
with vital health
and high stamina
brim in my being,
with bright wisdom
and spirited sparks
of speed at need.

My will is strong
and steers my way;
it guides me to goals
of glory and might.
It's hard and magical,
hallowing my life;
it's spiritual and focusing
to speed my work.

I make my way
— to Mead, Runes, and Grails —
as a sneaking serpent
and soaring eagle,
with awesome ᛏᚠᚾᚱᚾᛏ,
my excellent fetch,
as a powerful partner
on these potent quests.

For Gods and in Gilds
I grow and become,
and my efforts honor
the ancestors well!
As highest self,
a hero I'll be
and rightly rise
to reach Valhalla.

I'll drink in draughts
the dearest of meads
with lusty ᛏᚠᚾᚱᚾᛏ
and live forever.
To the home of heroes,
the highest of Folk,

aware, awakened,
ᚠᚨᚦᛒᚨᚱᚠ rises!

Fetch Call

With dark hair, pale eyes,
and dreamy white skin
in a slender form
of searing beauty,
fare forth my fetch
from that fimbul hall,
our home together
high on the tree.

Mead-cup maiden,
marching quickly,
embrace my being
with your brightest light.
Swan-white valkyrie,
soaring quickly,
journey in joy
and join me here.

In love and lust
I long for you;
for your runes and mead
I rown to you now.
Bring elder lore
of ancient days;
tell of my deeds and doom,
surge in my soul and mind,
come to my form and flesh.

Fetch Toasts

Ēalā ᛏᚠᚢᚱᚢᛏ,
my awesome fetch,
to thee I pour my praise!
By your glorious gift
of great initiation,
I am here tonight a hero,
I am here tonight in need.

Myrg ᛗᛊᛩᚢᛈᛣᛏ,
my mystery woman,
to thee I pour my praise!
The kith and kin
of my clan I honor
through you a link to that line,
through you who's lived in those lives.

Welgā ᚠᚡᚦᛩᚱᛁᚠᛗ,
my wodecraft muse
to thee I pour my praise!
As skald and scholar
I sculpt my words
to honor your inspirations
and honor our growth together.

Fetch Drápa

She is ᛏᚠᚢᚱᚢᛏ,
the Ale-Mystery:
my valkyrie wife
and valiant woman.
As ᛗᛊᛩᚢᛈᛣᛏ

she moves my soul;
as ᚠᚨᚦᛗᚱᛁᚠᛗ
my wode she stirs.

I called to ᛏᚠᚢᚱᚾᛏ:
"Come into my soul;
in the form of flesh
fly into my life.
Together we'll grow
and gain through love;
as partners paired,
our power is great."

ᛏᚠᚢᚱᚾᛏ came first
at August blessing
with a mighty milk stout
as the mead I offered.
My wode was stirred
by her warm embrace;
my soul had soared
on seeing her form!

Her other forms
also have wisdom:
as golden cone
she's ᚼᚱᚠᛏᛱᚠᛏᛱ hight,
as bold gray horse
she is ᛒᛁᚱᚷᚠᛗᚠᛏ.
Together they all
have glorious runes.

To the Tree she led me,
that tallest of yews:
I hung for its treasure;

she hallowed my work.
Roaring I took
the runes and fell;
she lifted me up
to live once more.

She is the Rúna
I rightly seek:
the Ale-Mystery,
my awesome maiden.

With seductive face
and darkest hair,
her slender form
and searing beauty
are only matched
by her excellent mind
and strength of spirit
that stirs my wode.

Her pale white skin
is pure and soft;
her icy pale eyes
have awed my heart.
In lover's form
as flesh she comes;
in spirit's form
she spurs my work.

My fetch within
is a fimbul lady:
the Ale-Mystery,
my awesome maiden.

Tall and sensuous,
her taste inspires.
She's caring, kind,
and quick to smile.
My woman of wyrd
brings wynn to my life;
the web she weaves
through work as a norn.

Learned and driven,
she lives as wode;
quick and clever,
she kens the mysteries.
The life she lives
enlightens all
with exemplary zeal
in the zone of earth.

Her fimbul fire
fuels my work;
the mead she brings
is the magic of wode.

We come together,
coupling often,
as a quivering quern
to quicken our lust.
Our sexual fire,
searing brightly,
is a pyre of power
for potent workings.

Mead and mystery
are married in us;

vital valknuts
with vigor we lay.
The world is changed
by our work in tandem;
the boons we bring
will benefit all.

Her spirit inspires
my spiritual growth;
the mead she brings
is the magic of wode.

As Gunnlöð and Óðinn,
together we've lain.
I bared my soul;
she brought me the horns.
As eagle I soar
in honor of her;
the might and main
of mead I pour.

My mead-cup maiden
demands her due;
she drives me to poems
and to pour those draughts.
As winsome wellspring
of wonderful staves,
she's filled my form
with fiercest wode.

Her glorious gift
is great initiation:
the craft of becoming
and cup of the grail.

Our bond was sealed
in my sitting-out;
the work was witnessed
by water and moon.

We grow and gain
together in quest,
on the road we ride
to runes and mead.
With wode for wings
we'll wend to Valhalla
as valkyrie maid
and mighty hero.

She'll bear to me
the brightest mead,
that dearest draught
drawn from Heiðrún.
In the home of heroes,
the highest of Folk,
with endless honor
ᛏᛚᚢᚱᚾᛏ shines!

The Work of Nine Doors

Initiation

I will to tell
the Work of the Doors,
that way of growth
on a wending road
and all the parts
on that awesome path
that aims to master
the might of Runes.

Energy with Form
and Order with Chaos
are the sought-for blends
by the seekers of Runes.
Through wisdom's work
on the way to Rûna,
the Self can gain
great initiation.

The Elder Fuþark
is the awesome spur:
four and twenty
are the twigs of blood.
These staves of strength
will start this work
and see it through
to success at last.

Rûna the mystery
is the rightful spur:

that singular secret
and its seeking out.
This steady beacon
will start this work
and see it through
to success at last.

To hang on the tree,
how is it done?
The making sacred
of self is the work.
A mighty tree
you must become
in the thousand days
of Thund's great work.

Listen here now
to the lays I sing
and hear the Runes
risted in speech.
With a keen mind,
ken these fine songs
and further the work
of the fimbul Doors.

These poems I brew
are potent draughts:
blood and honey
blended in craft,
fermented in kettles,
Kvasir's wisdom,
highest in proof,
potent for Runers.

Books

A bounty of lore
is in books you read.
Thus first you gain
a firm grounding
in objective forms,
before the subjective.
Then blend them together
and balance your work.

Learn the exoteric,
the lore of the runes,
knowledge from scholars,
skilled in their craft.
Learn the esoteric,
the lore of the runes,
knowledge from masters,
mighty in their craft.

Primary and secondary
are the sources you use:
the lore of skalds
and scholarly works
on gods and myths
both great and small.
They are awesome stories
for your understanding.

Knowledge of the soul
you seek and learn;
eke out that lore,
ancient and modern.
Knowledge of the worlds

you need and want:
the outer and inner
of Yggdrasil and Self.

Folktales and legends,
the forms they contain,
stories of magic
and the master game,
the culture of the Folk
and its famous heroes:
that poetry and prose
is powerful to know.

But learn the most
a love of reading,
a burning need
for books to read.
Your seeking of lore
leads to insights:
the objective fuels
and feeds the subjective.

Personal Analysis Diary

A personal analysis
you need to make:
a strong and stark
and steady look
at soul and self
to see with truth
the layers of your being
and learn them well.

Ponder the past,
present, and should
to know who you are
and need to become.
A census of self
you seek to make:
your manner of being,
both bright and murk.

You rightly pair
the runes with your traits,
and fathom the mysteries
you find in yourself.
Seek to discern
the sooth in your will;
that quest and work
will quicken your Self.

Put in practice
the pondering of self
by strengthening the bright
and balancing the murk;
the psyche's synthesis
you seek to complete
in riding the road
to runic mastery.

Concentration

You craftily train
your concentration
to give a focus
to flighty thoughts

and to find within
a fount of stillness,
that stead of magic
standing inside.

Steady and still
is the state of your sight:
the eyes of flesh
and the eyes of mind.
Your theater within
will thrive with practice.
Potent and internal,
'tis a power you need.

Secure in your center
though beset by storms:
such mastery gives
your mind the strength
to work in the world
the will of your Self.
Potent and external,
'tis a power you need.

Carve the Fuþark

Carve the runes
in the right order
to work the sought-for synthesis.
Stain them in flesh
by standing in the shapes;
strengthen your body with staves.

Breathe in air
with brightest runes;
store their essence in self.
See the staves
with sight of craft
in the eyes of lich and light.

Carve them in space,
carefully with gand;
send them strong and swift.
Carve them in air,
artfully with sound;
vibrate the staves with voice.

Carve them in wood,
carefully with sax;
stain the staves with will.
Carve them in mind
with crafty thoughts;
stain those staves in self.

Craft a poem
and compose it well;
rightly tally the runes.
Cast the staves
on a cloth of white;
learn the hidden layers.

'Tween tree and ring
and temple of flesh,
link the living staves.
Ride on rune-roads
by rowning the staves;
explore the worlds all-wide.

Carve and craft
and cast and breathe
and see and stain and stand
and rown and ride
to rightly know
the fimbul Fuþark Runes!

Breathing

The gift of Óðinn
is glorious önd,
so develop well
your vital breath.
Tally your breaths,
control them well
and voice the vowels
with vigor and mind.

Keeping them clean,
consonants are next;
with steady breathing
combine the sounds.
Then breathe for balance
bright runes and elements
to alter the inside
of your own universe.

Then going beyond
galdor and elements,
seek the power
of pure breathing;
with sacred syllable
center your mind

and feel the önd
flowing within.

Rune-Thinking

With mind and memory,
meditate on runes,
in all their aspects,
eagerly seek them:
name and stanza,
stave and number,
ideas and sound,
and deepest lore.

Then load the forms
with lore that's hidden
and link them well
with life today,
yet keep your focus
on the core of mystery
while following leads
to further knowing.

Ponder the poems,
the powerful staves,
that lore of old
left by masters.
Explore them well
to expand your knowledge
and lay the layers
for learning more.

With links established,
you strive for more,
riding rune-streams
to realms beyond.
Seeds you will find
and save for later;
some are senseless,
yet some are profound.

Then ponder pairs
and potent triads
of runes together
as gleaned from the row.
Wander the web
that weaves through them
and ardently travel
that endless path.

Then rightly gallop,
guided by Rûna:
ever and always,
onward you'll go
to eke out knowledge
and understanding
of that fimbul Word,
the Fuþark itself.

Standing-Work

Start the standings
with stillness first,
stay as a statue of ice.
Then practice the shapes

of the powerful runes:
stand in their steads and know.

Then learn the leek-fields
of the lyke's surroundings,
and channel their might and main.
Runic rivers
run through the body;
explore and feel their flow.

Form with hands
the holy runes
and strengthen your potent palms.
A magical medium
you make your body,
and work with the ancient words.

Then work by body
the will you choose
as a breathing, blood-filled tine.
With careful standings
and a crafty mind,
yourself and Midgard are moved.

Signing and Sending

Sign and send
sorcerous runes
as another tool of need.
Practiced often,
this power will grow;
start with hammer and hail.

With gand you grave
the glorious staves
in seemingly empty air,
but hurled with heart,
the hallowed signs
will work in the realms around.

Paired with Yew,
this potent work
will grow for further gain.
The inner and outer
are altered thus
through magical symbol might.

Galdor

Sing first the seeds,
the sounds of the runes,
imbue them with might and mind.
Then galdor their songs
and giving them voice,
fuse them together with form.

Next learn the legacy
left by the ancients:
the formulas found in stone.
Pour out the Alu
and its awesome power
and link the past to present.

Finally sing
songs you make new,
crafted for custom works.

Step in the stead
of the storied ancients
and in Midgard work your will.

Lots and Tines

Craft in wood
some wights with main:
four and twenty of twigs.
Those staves you cut
and stain with blood:
mysteries live in the lots.

To search your past,
present, and should
— the way of wyrd in your life —
upon the cloth
you cast the lots
and truly read them aright.

The runes you've cast:
the rede they give
is wise if well you read.
The web of wyrd
and its ways you seek
on the mighty path to mystery.

Craft in wood
some wights with main
to work your holy will.
With strength you use
the staves you've learned
in charms to change your life.

Cut from a tree
a tine of power
and surely shape its form;
carve the staves
and stain them well
with brightest blood and will.

From darkness is born
a being of magic
to faithfully work your will;
name and ørlög
are needed to doom
the wight with will and power.

When the wight's work
has wended its course,
finished with fail or gain,
a proper death
is its prudent due:
have it buried or burned.

Load them well,
the lots and tines;
from tree to wood goes wode.
Through balanced reading
blended with carving,
you'll receive and send the Runes.

The Yew-Work

Now I sing
a song of that work:
tending the tree within.

Strong it stands
on the estate of the soul;
grow it to wax in wisdom.

Fashion well
the forms to use
for the shining, shimmering wheels.
Cut and shape
the sure timbers
by often voicing the vowels.

Straight and tall
stand in practice;
be as the trunk of a tree.
To enable the axis,
the ash you sing,
and shine that shimmering light.

Yearn to become
the yew throughout,
and in your being rist its runes.
Well prepared,
powerfully do
with wisdom the work of yew.

Draw with roots
the darkest waters;
drink a draught from below.
Bring with branches
the brightest airs;
breathe a light from above.

The flow of force,
feel it continue

toward that middle wheel.
Order it outward,
aiming the power
to the worlds and wheels in the plane.

Eight of wheels
through awesome turning
feed to the middle their force.
Merging in Midgard,
the mighty center,
they fulfill that flow in self.

Now whirl that wheel
of worlds around you;
faster and faster they go.
With a turning mill
you train your mind
to focus and feel those realms.

Raise it up
to the realms above;
feed and fuel their might.
Lower it down
to the lands below;
feed and fuel their main.

Restore it to center
and stop its spin;
balance that might and main.
Breathe in well
and water your tree
to sow the seeds of growth.

Now array the roads
that ring the tree;
make them firm and fast.
Feel them well,
find their secrets,
and pair the roads with runes.

Then sing the Fuþark
to finish the work,
linking outer with inner.
The finished tree
is a fimbul tool
for wielding your magical will.

Seek Rûna

Seek Rûna
with serious intent
to work the sought-for synthesis,
but also seek
all her children
as a gift and guide to her.

In worlds without,
work to find her:
yearn for what's beyond
in dusty tomes
and deep waters
and the whole of mighty Midgard.

In worlds within,
work to find her:
seek for what's yourself

in states of mind
and steads of memory
and the whole of your hallowed being.

In worlds of flesh
work to find her:
look for what's alive
among the plants
and many animals
and all with spark of spirit.

Knowledge, insight,
and needful action
is the cycle she sets in motion.
Onward, upward,
always you'll go,
and forever *Reyn til Rúna!*

Blessing-Work

The magic of blessing
is a mighty galdor;
practice this work with wights.
Complex and hidden
are the powerful flows
that a blessing gift begets.

The harrow's space
is a whole universe;
the actions occur therein.
Hallowing marks
the holy stead;
the reading and rede make links.

A wight is welcomed
for weal with a call:
an act of esteem and honor.
Then mead is poured
for the mighty work
and filled with fimbul words.

Drink the power
in that draught and gain;
within the words will wax.
Then lay the power
on lyke and harrow;
without the words will wax.

Then give as gift
your galdor by pouring
that bowl to the being you called.
Thus wrought is the work
and wisely ended,
but listen for answers and learn.

Oft and well
offer blessings
to many sundry souls:
elves and dwarves,
etins and valkyries.
No being is out of bounds.

To the Gild's high gods
then gift your blessings:
both Woden and Freyja for weal.
Offer the bowl,
but not overmuch,
for always a gift seeks gain.

Road-Wending

Test the pathways
on the tree you've built:
a world with a world,
welded together.
You hear and see
with Huginn and Muninn:
while you're wending,
they'll whisper much.

The fimbul roads
have a fuþark each,
and a rightful rune
that rules as well.
Feeling them out,
find those mysteries
by careful thought
for three times each.

Then ride those roads
with their runic keys
to the wondrous worlds
that wait in the Yew.
Valued equally,
visit them all,
and angle along
on every path.

Gods and wild wights
you'll greet on your way;
their halls and homes
are hidden everywhere.
Both murk and bright

you must embrace
in exploring the worlds
by spying within.

Seið-Work

The Vanir's magic
is valued much,
so learn the arts
of Lady Freyja
for faring forth
to fabulous worlds
and saying sooth
of secret things.

Relax as a start;
release your tension.
On rhythmic sounds
then center your will.
Then outside your self,
seek to attune;
break the barriers
'tween body and things.

Let myne reflect
the mysteries beyond
in all the worlds
and every direction.
Fare to the world
that you find the best
and seek your warden
for sooth and knowledge.

Such seið is a start;
you may seek further.
'Tis a gate to magics
of greater main:
the shifting of shape,
as a shaman might,
and sexual seið
for sorcerous ends.

The Wode-Self

Your mightiest work
is the magical persona
that's used for greatest galdor.
You step in the stead
of strongest Asgard
to assume a godly self
and work as Óðinn would.

First you form
a physical image
through art of mindful eye.
Then make as well
a mental image,
an ego lacking limits,
and to both give might and main.

A name you take
to narrow your focus
in this glorious wode-filled work.
Choose it well,
for it changes your wyrd

and guides your growth ahead
to words and works beyond.

With runes and words,
you rightfully merge
the created souls with self:
"I, Erilaz,
of Asgard's kin,
now rown the runes like Óðinn,
filled with his fimbul might!"

Sitting Out

The final work
of the fimbul Doors
is seið through sitting out.
The soul of your fetch
you seek through a working:
a going out to go in,
a going in to go out.

For nine of hours
have needful silence,
and step to the working stead.
Oft meditate
on the aims of the work
and hallow at dusk this deed
with pride in past and clan.

In solemn vigil
seek the numen,
that essence from other worlds.
Then galdor to her,

your goddess within,
with total might and mind,
with full and holy heart.

Deeply drink
a draught to her
and recite a fimbul full.
Pour her a part
of that potent brew
along with lust for her,
along with love for her.

Sing a last song
for solid contact
then speak for a spell to her.
Gifts she gives,
and great wisdom:
her name and line with love,
your name and work of need.

Go back to the world,
bearing the wisdom
you gladly gained through union.
Then make a blessing
in her bright true name
and always honor this link,
and always honor her love.

Fulfillment

Through Thund's great work
of a thousand days
you've grown and gained

in Grímnir's might.
You've brought to balance
the bright and the murk
and won your way
on Woden's road.

In a bounty of books
and your being within,
many of mysteries
you've made your own.
The worlds you know;
now wield their power.
Your Self you've changed
through seeking Rûna.

When well you've waxed
with wode and fetch,
fall back from the tree,
unbound at last
to work your will
in the world of Midgard,
through knowledge, insight
and needful action.

Both write and read
the runes with skill;
galdor and cast
to guide your life.
For wisdom and weal,
work with the Yew,
both Tree without
and Tree within.

The runes you've carved
and Rûna you've sought,
but ever keep on
that awesome quest,
for much remains.
Remember always
the road to the runes
does run forever.

Sjálfsljóðin

The Elder Fuþark

The bright runes are
a boon to my work
of creating wholeness
and healing order.
The staves of self
I seek to strengthen;
for steadfast footing
the Fuþark I sing.

Fehu is first,
the force mobile.
Uruz is the ox
that urges one on.
Þurisaz is the thorn,
but Thor is stronger.
Ansuz is Óðinn,
the awesome god.

Raiðo is rhythm
and the riding wagon.
Kenaz is the keen
and crafty fire.
Gebo is gift
and good to receive.
Wunjo is wynn,
and wisdom it requires.

Hagalaz is the hail,
and hard it falls.

Nauðiz is need,
the narrow resistance.
Isa is the ice,
the awesome stillness.
Jera is the year,
the yearned-for harvest.

Æhwaz is the yew,
the ash of needles.
Perþro is the power
of play with the lots.
Algiz is the elk
and the awesome valkyrie.
Sowilo is the sun,
the sought-for light.

Tiwaz is Týr;
trust him for victory.
Berkano is the birch,
bright with leaves.
Ehwaz is the equine
and an eager partner.
Mannaz is man,
Midgard's adornment.

Laguz is the lake;
that liquid is deep.
Iŋwaz is Freyr,
the earth's lord.
Dagaz is day,
the dearest of lights.
Oþala is the ancestors,
the oldest estate.

The Self is stirred
by this song of order,
and the work of growth
begins in earnest.
I go on to sing
the songs of my traits
strengthening the bright
and balancing the murk.

The Odian Path

I aim to follow
the Odian Path —
in three of things
I thrive and grow.
Because the quarry
in the quest is Rûna,
in thoughts and words
and works I live.

A gleaming Thought
I glimpsed in my mind:
the spark is kindled
by speaking Kenaz,
heightened and fueled
by Hagalaz and Mannaz;
a firestorm of Thoughts
flared in response.

The seed of a Word
I sought to raise:
the grain is planted
by galdoring Iŋwaz,

broken and grown
by Berkano and Ansuz;
a bounty of Words
I won in the harvest.

A mighty Work
I willed to create:
the engine is built
by uttering Tiwaz,
throttled and raced
by Þurisaz and Raiðo;
a train of Works
trailed behind.

In wisdom great
I waxed and thrived:
from thought to thought
by thoughts I fared,
from word to word
by words I fared,
from work to work
by works I fared.

My Quest for the Runes

I sing of the quest
that quickens my life
and the fimbul runes
that rightly further it
Myself to myself
in song I give,
seeking mysteries
and might for life.

I carve Æhwaz
to climb the Tree
and hang upon
its holy trunk;
I rist Algiz
to readily explore
the worlds it bears
in branches and roots.

I galdor Gebo
to give myself
as a gift to myself
that I gladly receive.
I rist Raiðo
to rightly quest,
seeking mysteries
in the self and world.

Fuþark's spell
spurs the work,
that awesome fusion
of energy and form;
Rûna's spell
spurs the work,
that awesome combine
of order and chaos.

To learn from Masters
I look to the Gild;
my words and works
of worth I share.
Mysteries and mead
I mix together

for self's synthesis
and soul's initiation.

By risting this song
and singing the quest,
right and real
are the runes I gain.
In the Songs of Self
a saga is carved,
and I quarry the staves
that quicken my life.

My Quest for the Mead

I sing of the quest
that quickens my soul
and the fimbul runes
that rightly further it.
Awesome Óðrœrir
I earnestly seek,
to deeply drink
that draught of might.

The mead I seek
through magical quest;
in hidden realms
these runes I chant.
I galdor Sowilo
to go as a serpent,
over and under
the etins' road.

I sing Berkano
and breach the enclosure,
reaching the cavern
keeping the mead.
I sing Ehwaz
and eagerly lay
the etin woman
warding the mead.

I utter Ansuz,
and Óðrœrir I drink;
the power of poetry
pours through my soul.
I sing Jera
to soar as an eagle,
bearing that booty
back in my flight.

I utter Oþala,
and in Óðinn's hall
I reach and greet
gods and heroes.
I galdor Gebo
and gift the mead,
pouring out poems
with pride and honor.

The mead I seek
through much of study;
in manifest realms
these runes I chant.
I utter Æhwaz
for eager spirit,

the fire of life
that fuels my love.

I galdor Oþala
to gain from ancestors
learning and language,
leading to skill.
I utter Ansuz
for awesome synthesis:
the work of skald
and scholar I blend.

By brewing this song
and singing the quest,
might and main
and mead I gain.
In the Songs of Self
a saga is poured,
and I quaff the draught
that quickens my soul.

Three Sovereign Virtues

A mighty song
I sing of virtues;
three are supreme,
peerless, and sovereign.
Essential to have,
they help my quest,
riding the road
to Runes and Mead.

These valued virtues
I venture to name:
Inspiration of Óðinn,
awesome to know;
Memory of Mímir,
mighty to have;
Thought of Hœnir,
highly prized.

To win for my wode
the winsome mead,
Ansuz and Dagaz
and Algiz I sing.
I draw the drink;
the draught is strong.
I pour the poetry;
potent are my words.

To make in my myne
memory unfailing,
Uruz and Laguz
I utter with Mannaz.
The flow gushes up,
forth from the wells;
knowledge and wisdom
I win from the deep.

To have in my hugh
the highest of thoughts,
Kenaz and Hagalaz
I carve with Mannaz.
I shape the sure
and shining forms,

brightly born
in my being's depths.

Essential to self,
I seek these virtues:
mysteries of the head
and a help to the Work.
The first of functions
I fulfill with skill
for great becoming
and glorious being.

Nine Noble Virtues

A mainful song
I sing of virtues;
nine they number,
noble they be.
Useful to have,
they help my quest,
riding the road
to Runes and Mead.

I bless with Dagaz
for brightest Truth;
for leading my life
that light is a guide.
I name Nauðiz
for needed Self-Reliance;
my resources within
are a ready friend.

I galdor Isa
for good Discipline;
governing myself
is the greatest power.
I carve Kenaz
for keen Industriousness;
doing as dwarves
drives my success.

I utter Æhwaz
for awesome Perseverance;
enduring as yew
is useful deeply.
I utter Uruz
for aurochs' Courage;
the boldness of beast
is best for action.

I carve Tiwaz
for trusty Fidelity
to fetch and Self
and folk and gods.
I galdor Gebo
for good Hospitality:
a gift for a gift
in glad exchange.

I sing Sowilo
for essential Honor;
my will and words
and works accord.
Value and victory
these virtues give;

needful to know
are the nine I've sung.

Six-Fold Goal

A galdor of goals
I give in song;
six their sum,
I seek in earnest.
Though more I have,
mainful these be;
there is shining success
in their sure seeking.

I shape Raiðo
for surest Right;
justice and reason
are my journey's rule.
I utter Ansuz
for excellent Wisdom;
a drink from that well
is the dearest friend.

I stain Þurisaz
for strongest Might,
to hold what I have
and harry for more.
I bless with Jera
for a bountiful Harvest
of wealth and health,
a help to my work.

I name Oþala
for needful Frith:
order and freedom
aid my workings.
I carve Wunjo
for keenest Love;
my life is powered
with pleasure and lust.

With runes these goals
I reach in glory,
and they brew the mead
brimming within.
In seeking these six
this song has furthered
the greater goals
of glory beyond.

The Will

A mighty will
I mean to have
for seeking Self
on my self's long road.
Will is the steersman
that steadies the course;
that portion of soul
is synthesis-guiding.

The will is charged
with choosing well —
the task it takes
on the team of self.

I sing for my will
a song of strength,
raising it high
with the runes I chant.

By narrow Nauðiz
my need is strengthened;
mighty it makes
my magical will.
By Tiwaz my troth
is trained in faith —
the spur and spark
of my spiritual will.

By Þurisaz my will
is awakened to action;
I aim for deeds
of daring and might.
The cold of Isa
clears my mind;
filled with frost,
focus I gain.

I kindle with Æhwaz
an awesome fire;
that holy wood
hallows my will.
The light of Sowilo
I seek and love;
sure it makes
my shining will.

My will is stronger
by the staves I've sung;

better choices
and changes I make.
Powerful plans
with purpose I lay —
I craftily guide
their carrying out.

The Fetch

For gaining glory
great is my need,
and in many forms
my fetch I call.
I utter Ehwaz
for eager partners,
and more of runes
I rist by kind.

I galdor Algiz
to gain my valkyrie,
a warrior woman
wise and faithful.
In lover's form
as flesh she comes;
in spirit's form
she spurs my work.

I galdor Sowilo
to gain my serpent
and eagerly wax
in Ófnir's ways.
My fetch of wyrm
fuels my wisdom

and guides me sneaking
in seething deep.

I galdor Jera
to gain my eagle
and eagerly wax
in Arnhöfði's ways.
My fetch of bird
fuels my boldness
and guides me soaring
in searing sky.

I galdor Uruz
to gain my horn —
might it proffers;
main it pours.
My fetch of cone
fuels my craft;
in a life of wode,
my work it inspires.

I galdor Oþala
to gain my kinfetch
with its mighty wyrd
and mainful ørlög,
seeking to do
my ancestral duty;
burden and blessing
are blended with soul.

I utter Wunjo
for added harmony;
joined in purpose,
our power expands.

Our quest's way
is quickened well;
together we ride
for Runes and Mead.

The Önd

For spiritual power
to spur my workings,
my önd from Óðinn
I aim to strengthen.
For breath with main
— a mighty boon —
I expel this spell,
and speak in verse.

Ansuz I breathe,
and the air of being,
filling my lungs,
furthers my life;
force of spirit
flows from my speech;
in mindful exhale
my might is holy.

Uruz I utter
with Ehwaz next,
Isa after
and Oþala last;
to mindful chant
— charged with main —
awesome value
is added by vowels.

Mannaz I hum,
hearing its main;
Man furthers
Fimbultýr's might.
Óðinn's gift
— glorious önd —
my sturdy galdor
greatly strengthens.

The Lich

The health of my lich
I labor to hold
and greatly wax
to gain in life;
for work and will
my wagon in Midgard
serves me well
on my way to glory.

For vital power
this verse I sing:
for stamina and strength
I stain Uruz;
for youthful vigor
I voice Laguz;
for bodily fire
I bloody Kenaz.

To rise with energy
from restful sleeping,
I rist and stain
Raiðo and Iŋwaz —

my sleep is still
and restores my being;
I rise by Berkano
brightly at dawn.

I stress my muscles
and stretch my joints;
I sing Nauðiz
for needful resistance
with Uruz for muscles
and Æhwaz for joints —
benefits to body
are brought by my work.

For balance and intake
I utter these staves:
by Wunjo I balance
my body's weight;
by Ansuz I clean
the air I breath;
by Uruz I manage
the meals I eat.

Health I have
and health I keep
by the strong staves
I've stained and sung.
With lust for life
I live in Midgard;
my life is long
and leads to growth.

Speed

Swiftness I seek
for successful ways —
the speed of the horse
for sprinting at need
and ready stamina
to rightly sustain
a lightning pace
on my lengthy path.

For galloping great
I galdor Ehwaz
and rist that rune
for running quick
and stain that stave
for a steady pace;
the mysteries of speed
are mighty indeed.

My horse's running
is helped by runes:
Þurisaz spurs it
to speedy starting,
healing with haste
is helped by Uruz,
and eager learning
by Ansuz is hurried.

My rate of mind
is raised by Mannaz,
Dagaz accelerates
the dawn of awareness,
and my essential essence

75

Æhwaz quickens.
Bolstered with runes,
I ride with speed.

I partner with fetch
for further power;
with Algiz I awaken
my winsome steed.
That holy horse —
I hearken her rede.
Together with fylgja,
fast I will be.

Tongues

Next I sing
a song of words:
staves for writing,
staves for reading,
staves for speaking,
staves for hearing,
in the many tongues
of Teutonic folk.

Poetry and prose
— a powerful flow —
I seek to write
by singing Ansuz.
Staves and secrets
strewn on pages
I seek to read
by singing Ansuz.

With powerful voice
and pleasing sounds,
I seek to speak
by singing Ansuz.
Staves that fly,
streaking in air,
I seek to hear
by singing Ansuz.

Fluent and true
in the tongues of the folk
I seek to become
by singing Ansuz:
writing, speaking,
reading, and hearing
in the many tongues
with might like Óðinn.

Joy and Happiness

Shining in my life
is a sure light;
the spirit of joy
is a spark in my soul.
I rist with sound
and sing those runes
that place in my heart
happiness and peace.

The light of joy
lifts my mind
when with wisdom
Wunjo I chant.

The play of Perþro
is a potent tonic
for charging mood
with cheerful main.

Calm and mellow
I keep relaxed,
taking my ease
by tracing Iŋwaz.
For pathways long
I linger upon
the power of Jera
and the patience it yields.

The light of Sowilo
lifts the darkness
within and without —
always it shines.
The power of Dagaz
is dear to the self
and brings to my heart
the hope that I need.

Seeking the runes
raises my being;
my heart is heightened
by the holy staves.
Happiness and hope
I have with joy
by singing this song
and seeking to live.

Fear

To face my fears
and find my courage,
this mainful spell
I speak with might
against intrinsic
and internal fears,
against extrinsic
and external fears.

I sing Uruz
for awesome courage;
that beast is steady,
bellowing fiercely.
I call out Tiwaz
for courage to act;
a resolute deed
He did for right.

I name Ansuz
to know my fears
and Dagaz to show them
in shining light.
Swiftly is drained
the swamp of delusions;
fewer are the fears
I first reckoned.

To face the fears
that are found within,
lurking in the deepest
and darkest steads,
I name Laguz

to know myself
and embrace the waters
brimming within.

To face the fears
that are found without,
lurking in the world
and waking life,
I name Mannaz
to know my fellows
and embrace humanity
brightly in Midgard.

The axis of forever
and the orbit of time —
their conquering requires
courage and resolve.
Æhwaz frees me
from fear of death;
Jera frees me
from fear of life.

Fears within
and fears without
are rightly settled
by risting this song;
paranoid delusions
leave my mind,
and a flood of courage
fills my being.

A Call to Action

I'm timid and shy
when tortured by doubt;
manifold are
the murky staves
that mire in a quag
my quickness of mind
and bring my being
abruptly to idle.

The stillness of Isa
can strangle the self;
its murky form
can mire the will.
I rown those runes
for rising to action
and melting the ice
with eager response.

In thinking thoughts
is the threat of excess —
I stain Tiwaz
to stem the flow
and speak Þurisaz
to spur certainty;
I quickly choose
a required choice.

Perþro's pleasures
I powerfully sway
to Sowilo's sign,
a certain light;
by Berkano's beckoning

my being is changed,
and with Raiðo's rhythm
I rightly act.

The need of Nauðiz
is narrow on the self —
by heeding hard
and heavy force,
I form and kindle
a crafty fire:
a brightly blazing
burning desire.

The ice is melted
by the mighty fire,
and my thoughts are still
and strongly focused;
My lot aligns
with light from the sun,
and my soul as a thorn
is thrusted forward.

With birth in birch
I burst into action,
riding onward
to realms of doing;
my mind is drained
of dreary murk,
and willful and daring
are my works and deeds.

Communication

I speak this spell
to spur my talk,
to sharpen skills
for shaping words
to utter to elm
and ash in wisdom,
and to converse with folk
with vigor freely.

I rist Kenaz
for keen charisma
and galdor Gebo
for glad exchange.
I utter Ansuz,
aiming for grace;
the might of Mannaz
musters rapport.

I call on Wunjo
for wise accord;
with folk and friends
I freely speak.
For using silence
I sing Iŋwaz;
I wield with wisdom
this way of being.

Ehwaz I utter
for empathy's help;
partnership's power
proffers trust.
With Oþala I finish:

this final stave
gives a setting
for the sense of events.

Sharp are my skills
and sure is my manner
in risting this song
sung with runes.
Surging success
in social life
quickly follows
quality staves.

Sex

I sing this song
of sexual life
to bring to my bed
a beautiful partner;
pleasures of the flesh
are a favored part
of a fulfilling life
lived in Midgard.

I name Nauðiz
and my need is kindled;
that fire of will
fuels my success,
and a special need
is sparked inside
the winsome woman
I want to have.

I carve Kenaz
for keen attraction,
starting connections
and strengthening lust.
The urge for expression
in the act of sex
gives us a flood
of fierce desires.

I utter Algiz
for aid from my fetch;
my valkyrie emerges
in the maid I desire,
increasing her lust
and carnal need;
she seeks my flesh
for sweet release.

I galdor Þurisaz
to aggressively act,
working my will
towards a union.
My thorn of might
mainfully thrusts;
my doings made
its deeds occur.

I galdor Gebo
for glad exchange —
awesome pairings
with an eager partner.
A gift for a gift
each gains in sex:

the joy of blending
we both receive.

A special spark
in my spirit is put
by the joining of flesh
in joyful union.
By knowing a woman
my knowledge of mystery
in this work of will
and wode has increased.

Wealth and Income

Gold I seek
regardless of source:
work or investment,
windfall or dole.
Having wealth
helps my Work;
earned or unearned,
it is honored the same.

My spending is frugal
so funds will last —
a two-fold test
I try for things:
What do I need?
What can I use?
Wealth with wisdom
I wisely spend.

For room and board,
blót and sumbel,
travel and gatherings,
tools and books,
school for grads,
and skaldcraft great
much of money
must be gathered.

For fees and funds
in fortunate amounts
to freely flow
fast to my accounts
and for fuel and fire
to fulfill my quest,
I formulate Fehu —
that form is best.

The receiving and spending
of silver is helped
by rightly risting
runes to assist:
inherited Oþala
helps in earning;
that spiritual legacy
spurs my living.

Perþro's power
pulls in the Well:
through the web of wyrd
wealth it proffers.
Æhwaz draws,
ever from the tree,

income throughout
all the worlds.

Wealth to me flows
for the Work I do
though cause and effect
unclear remain;
balanced are the books
by the bread I gain;
my living will make
mysterious links.

This song I sing
is serious indeed;
that flow of funds
is fuel for life.
But the flow within
of fire as well
for the runic road
is rightly needed.

Ancestry and Community

An awesome song
of ancestry I sing —
that dear mystery
is mighty indeed:
in kith and kin
and the clan's deep roots,
the folk and its heritage
are famed and holy.

A mainful song
of community I sing —
that dear mystery
is mighty indeed:
the family and friends
who fit in my life;
the people and places
and the purposes they have.

I galdor Oþala;
that great heritage
— a strengthening stave —
steadies my soul.
A god-sprung life,
the legacy of ghost,
and a foundation firm
are fortunate to have.

Wunjo generates
joy for the work;
my kith and kin
it keeps together.
With Perþro's power
I plunge in the Well,
eagerly seeking
Arfur and Siður.

With kindred folk
I feast and blót,
and family forms
a footing for life.
Community adds
might to my work;

I mingle well
with mainful wynn.

This spell strengthens
the spirits of ancestors;
their manifold might
magnifies my life.
Their memories I honor
with mainful effort,
traditional duty,
and deeds of might.

Self-Actualization

My final song
fulfills the rest
through heart and mind
and helps to make
the might and main
I mean to win
in a life I love
and live to have.

For seeking my Self
I sing Hagalaz;
that corn within
I call upon.
That grain it grows
and gives me food;
its pattern provides
vital power.

I blend in my being
the brightest fire
through clever craft
with clearest ice;
the seed of Self
inside is opened,
the seed of Self
inside is grown.

A Word I heard —
it waits inside,
that Work of Will
I want to do.
For its quest I'm readied
by quickening Self
and staining inside
my soul the Runes.

Now are sung
my songs of might;
their runes are risted
and reddened with main.
In writing and singing
my soul is strengthened;
by seeking these runes
my Self I become.

Runecraft: A New Rúnatal

The Challenge

The gar-wielder has a ghost of runes,
so seek sovereignty to give Self its boons!
I sing this song from the sage's stool
at the Well of Wyrd for the waxing trees.
Right rede I give, rendered fully,
to aid the ash who aims for glory
to hang on the ash and hallow his Self
to wield the ash as Woden does.

009   I tell the tale — with tallies included —
that belongs to all who lift the runes
from darkness deep to daylight's heights.
First was Woden, foremost seeker,
born of Bestla, Bölþorn's daughter,
and sired by Borr, son of Búri,
fully fusing the forms all three
that first emerged from the fire and ice
that turned together in time's beginning;

018   thus three he was. Thirsting fiercely
and acting only by inner patterns,
the brothers' rebellion then broke the world.
From baleful body he rebuilt the realms
with graceful glory in a girding tree.
Sensing mystery, unsatisfied yet,
craving wisdom, he climbed that wood.
For nights all nine he knew that he hung,
working his wyrd on that windy tree,

027   whose roots do run through realms unknown.
By gar he was gored, since gar he'd master,

92

and the runes began on that reddened gar
and there they will end. That is the way
for an ash on ash, by an ash wounded,
to give the Self a gift of self
and lay a link to the luminous pole.
Blessed with no bread, nor brimming horn,
at last he looked below those roots,

036 fiercely screaming, finding Rûna,
the singular secret he sought to grasp.
He took her whole with entire being
yearning a union that would yield him gnosis.
Ultimate ecstasy and awe he gained
from that glimpse of death on the gallows tree.
Then back he fell, to bear his gar
and wield its might o'er the Well and Tree,
through Runes returned from realms below.

045 From Mímir he learned mighty songs nine
by mastering self with the main of runes.
A draught he drank of the dearest mead
from that wondrous grail, Wode-Stirrer hight.
Then free at last, he flourished with life,
waxing greatly in wisdom's gifts.
A thought got a thought by a thought for him;
a word got a word by a word for him;
a work got a work by a work for him.

054 I heard tell of this as a trail to power;
thus I was also eager for mysteries
and would wield my gar for works of glory.
By gar wounded and given to Self,
I waxed with wode, that welcome might,
that raging fury and rising fire
felt in ecstasy and found in poems.
I saw the secret that Sigtýr found

and realized my work on the road unending.
063   It started my path, so it starts my tallies.
Rûna the Mystery is the rightful source
of the runes we rown to raise our Selves.
Ever and always with effort seek her
in worlds without, in worlds within,
and in forms of flesh that are found between.
So call to her with clearest mind,
as Woden would in want for Freyja,
for the power and pleasure her path will bring,
072   if you keep your courage in carrying on.

The Tally of Staves

From a single glimpse of that great secret,
my old self died in agony deep;
I found it fit for feeding ravens,
that hungry pair hidden inside;
around me then the ring unfolded,
emerging out from the mighty source.
Here I tally the haul I took,
those excellent twigs all twenty-four;
081   in my Self I stained their sacred lore.
Fehu is Fee that was formerly cattle,
rustled by heroes from robber barons,
and gold that's gained in glory from dragons.
'Tis dealt by drightens for a doom that's best,
to keep a frith that's clear of feuds.
As flowing fire, it fuels the worlds,
both outer and inner, in aiming for life.
This beast is tame and birthed in the garth,
090   a source for the man who seeks the refined.
Uruz is Aurochs, the ominous bull

faced by the brave in a fight to the death
to test their vigor and virile might.
The essential seed of sexual love
contains its essence in a tiny squirt,
and so does drizzle that drops from the sky,
fertilizing fields and flushing the dross.
This beast is wild and birthed in the moors,

099   a source for the man who seeks the primal.
Þurisaz is Troll, and it threatens harm
in reckless rage with ravenous action.
The passive thorn is a peril as well;
for unwary ones, it waits in ambush.
Their mighty force, in Mjöllnir's head,
is wielded by Thor to ward the good,
but 'tis hard for heroes to handle well.
'Tis often evil, this awesome being,

108   a greater-than-human grim phenomenon.
Ansuz is Ancestor, an Aesir god;
Woden is listed as one par excellence,
the master of words and martial fury.
The oak is best for building within
the firmest will to follow his path,
and ale is best for altering wyrd
by writing runes with unrivaled might.
'Tis often good, this awesome being,

117   a greater-than-human glorious noumenon.
Raiðo is Wagon, and riding as well,
on the lengthy road that leads to Self,
ever spiraling in endless cycles.
By holding to right, a healthy order
is built through turnings of bright and dark.
When wheels and axles are well aligned,
rede for the road is readily heard.

This craft of construction, careful synthesis,

126   manifests ice in its myriad forms.
       Kenaz is Torch, the carried light,
       bringing brightness to the boundless dark
       and serving the will of the seeker's way.
       Spinning the drill will spark its deeds,
       through flame without and flame within,
       but when wild in body as upwelling bale,
       it forms a sore with force of decay.
       This craft of destruction, careful analysis,

135   manifests fire in its myriad energies.
       Gebo is gift, a golden exchange;
       both liege to lord and life to the gods
       are bound in frith by this boon and law.
       Gained on gallows was a glorious spark
       that Woden gave to wood made human.
       By sovereign gar that cycle of gifts
       was started first and is strengthened best.
       This fimbul force, fueling communities,

144   is the outward basis of ordered society.
       Wunjo is Joy, the welcome end
       of work in the world and work in the Self
       when sores and sorrows are ascended over.
       Profitable pasture powers this striving
       by the area opened if edged rightly,
       and one's work will wax if the wolf of desire
       is carefully fed and kept in limits.
       This fimbul force, fueling our lives,

153   is the inward basis of ordered society.
       Hagalaz is Hail, a harrowing trauma,
       but planted with care, 'tis precious corn
       and the nurturing water needed for growth.
       A hardened hedge will help against

this sickness of snakes that's sent from above,
and the holy horn will hallow the soul
for seeking ascent from a sundered state.
This woe outside works its magic
162   by forcing change in physical life.
Nauðiz is Need, a narrow restraint,
and a force that's felt fully within;
it helps the most if heeded early.
The hub of a wheel holds it together,
despite the stress from spinning quickly,
and the clawing nail is clipped often
to restrain the growth of destruction's ship.
This woe inside works its magic
171   by inspiring change in spiritual life.
Isa is Ice, created from water;
a folly to fey men, famously gleaming,
though it roofs and stills the roiling waves.
This first material, when fixed as iron,
is made by dwarves into mighty treasures,
and the excellent one can own and wield
its force as a bridge to the fimbul gods.
Natural freezing lets needed rest
180   occur in the world at the cost of growth.
Jera is Year, the yearned-for harvest
in the annual cycle for earning wealth,
but proper planting comes prior to it.
Yeast will make yare the yield of malt
as the toil of time will turn the crops
till the stroke of a scythe stops the growing,
bringing the bounty back for the winter.
Natural ripening lets needed action
189   occur in the world at the cost of leisure.
Æhwaz is Yew, an ominous wood

that hoards a fire in its hallowed roots,
but 'tis joy for the stead that it stands upon,
and for sending will to soar over worlds,
a bow is best when built from this wood.
Its deeds are a light in the dark of existence,
and timeless if told in the tales of poets.
This coniferous tree has numinous main,
198   revealing the work of the vital eternal.
Perþro is Pear, a pleasant wood
for carving a cup to cast the lots
and the spirit of wyrd spoken in sumbel.
Its path of heroes is prowess-testing,
leading to ascent and sacred life,
and pulling the plow prepares a furrow
in the deep darkness for doom-seeking.
This deciduous tree has seasonal life,
207   revealing the work of the vital rebirth.
Elhaz is Elk with excellent horns
and a noble beast that nibbles the leaves
of the worldly tree for wisdom's gain.
Temples take part in its truest essence
by holding the highest in the here and now,
and so does the swan, a symbol for valkyrie
that is grim to grasp though it gives protection.
This supernal principle in a place terrestrial
216   is a polar guide for the profit of seekers.
Sowilo is Sun, the sailor's grace,
a shining wheel, a shield of clouds,
the light of the lands, and the limit of ice.
This jewel is a stone, the joy of perfection,
the greatest grail that is gained in quest,
but the snake is seen in the sun that's black,
a sign it was slain and consumed by the hero.

This supernal principle in a place celestial
225　　is solar guide for the glory of seekers.
Tiwaz is God, with a treelike column;
with craft his courage secured the wolf;
his right is rendered through rational order.
His loyalty to life and the light of truth
is the might he wields for community good,
and a certain sign in the cycling sky
is his polar star with a place that's fixed.
The transcendent sky, his source and home,
234　　bears his nature though embracing earth.
Berkano is Goddess, the Birch mistress,
attired in splendor like her special tree;
she is verdant, vital, and vigorous youth.
This bright one bears the rebirthing secret;
growth from the ground is her gift to Man.
By her help a bridge is hurried across,
though trolls are looking for lives to take.
The immanent earth, her origin and home,
243　　betrays her nature though touching sky.
Ehwaz is Horse, an excellent partner
for briskly moving o'er boundless space,
the most treasured beast that's tamed by Man.
The boar is wild in the border realms,
though ridden by gods who rule its power.
Both fared across the fence 'tween worlds,
though one had strained for the wall's building.
This effective being of physical might
252　　is close to the gods and kens their will.
Mannaz is Man, the middle being
gifted by Woden for the gladsome work
of raising Midgard in runic design.
The moon measures his mortal life,

an ever-reminder of endless rebirth,
but the golden mead is a glimpse of magic:
with wode one wields the wyrding main.
This active being of intellect's might,
261   must open his ears and eyes to the gods.
Laguz is Liquid, the lake's substance,
the blood of Ymir, the bounding falls,
and the ground of fish where gold is hidden.
The leek will grow to lofty status,
pure and shining like the proud hero.
The summons they give is to secret and quest:
to plumb the depths and push to the heights.
The infinite sea is awe-inspiring,
270   and organic growth is gained with it.
Iŋwaz is Hero, an earthly god;
the wending wain works his magic,
but the seasons' cycle will send it away.
Grief goes often with great initiation,
trials of detachment, and return with change,
but the fertile meadow is a field of growth,
for oak from acorn or for ears of wheat.
The infinite earth is awe-inspiring
279   and godly growth is gained with it.
Dagaz is Day, the dearest light,
sent from the sun yet seen in the moon,
the mighty mixing of measurer and drighten.
Dough will double from deeds of yeast:
fermenting leads to mysteries' growth.
Total twilight is a true paradox
that's neither day nor dark of night.
Time is limited by this liminal rune,
288   and so are the heavens circling on high.
Oþala is Estate, the ancestor's gift:

by land we're linked to the lives of old
and by customs carried across the years.
A river mouth will run to the sea,
joining the middle to a journey's path.
but inner from outer by edge is marked,
in people, tribes, and proud nations.
The earth is limited by this ending rune
297   and so are the tribes, separate yet true.

The Tally of Songs

These staves are a tool to establish one's truth,
so back unbound, being renewed,
I rebuilt my Self with the boons I gained.
I saw that onward I ever must seek
and was led to the songs that Sigtýr learned
from the mighty son of his mother's father:
they sovereignize self and make scepter of gar.
Now I tally those needful tunes,
306   a sequence of might that is sung with runes.
The first of songs is found in death.
Soul is seated and seen among roots,
an unconscious part that's kept in the dark.
Bring to the light its burden early,
to lessen its weight and lift it up,
like Baldur's return from the bonds of Hel.
As subtle body for psychic aspects,
rebirth it awaits in abodes of stillness,
315   though long it lingers in a lyke unburnt.
The second of songs is a secret rune.
Fetch can be found in forms that are three:
human, animal, and holy shapes.
This store of ørlög has estate's power;

'tis risky to grasp, but rightful embrace
is always good in the end though hard.
'Tis most like Freyja or mighty Rûna,
unique to each on the needful quest,
324   and is sought on the edge of the other songs.
The third of songs enthralls the form.
Hyde is the glue that holds together
and the base for building the body's shape;
'tis most like dwarves for making treasures.
Picture power will point its work
in fashioning forms, fimbul or subtle,
that work like bodies for the will to enter.
In the lyke that's linked, it leaves its gains
333   for harm or health or hallowing work.
The fourth of songs is a faculty sought.
Luck is valued by the living man;
'tis personal power, appended to Self,
for working the hyde of the world for gain,
and for shifting shape it's the surest way.
Deeds and doings of daring and right
will strengthen this store of stately wealth.
This might and main can amend the Self,
342   and is closest to fetch, keeping it fed.
The fifth of songs is the form at center.
Lyke lives only in the limits of Midgard,
yet 'tis gateway grand to glorious worlds.
Good looks and blood were given by Lóðurr,
so hold them whole for hallowed works,
as the other eight are aided by this.
Whether burned or buried, rebirth is affected
by the physical form's final ending,
351   and once it is left, no way leads back.
The sixth of songs is serious indeed.

Myne is memory, the mast for thought,
and a well whose water is weirdly deep,
with a source outside the self's knowledge.
Its head will tell of hidden tidings,
and with Mímir's Mead from a mighty pledge,
its mirror reflects fimbul mysteries.
This raven's droop is rightly dreaded
360   and mourned the most by men and gods.
The seventh of songs is seen in the air.
Önd is the breath that enters the body,
the gift of Woden that gives it life.
Divine and vital, it pervades existence:
an essential substance, unseen by fools.
Runic spirits, riding the air,
can enter through it to energize Self.
To higher being it's a helpful bridge,
369   from Midgard to Asgard for mighty ascent.
The eighth of songs is excellent indeed.
Hugh is the mind, the hoard of thinking,
a raven that flies and roams the world,
but hold it focused for higher work.
If whole and bright, it handles the blood twigs,
but without memory, it'll let others decide.
'Tis a fire that dissolves with fimbul zeal
in seeking answers, but it seldom congeals
378   if left alone to leap unchecked.
The ninth of songs is the needful zenith:
Wode is worked with for the will's magic.
'Tis Hœnir's gift to human life,
but follow its master on his fimbul path.
Names are needed to know its power;
choose them with care to change your wyrd.
Experienced in rage or the speech of poets,

the uplift it brings is an awe with main
387 and the way to Valhöll for the waxing Self.
For trees these songs are tallied thus,
that the tree within is trained for the work
of mastering Self for commanding the gar,
though the yew without is yet ahead.
So sing them oft, that the Self may gain
in true knowledge and continue the quest.
With these songs for Self, I sought a draught
of poetry's power, poured from a grail:
396 a welcome mead to wax my main.
For **Wode-Stirrer** I worked some bale;
with gar as auger I gained the mountain,
sneaking inside in serpent's form
to the woman within to work my magic.
Together we got the greatest ale
that's best if brewed in your being's depths.
It shook my tree from shining top
to darkest roots as I dared escape
405 in eagle's form to awesome heights.
Then fertile I became through ferment within,
waxing in wisdom from wellsprings deep,
growing and thriving in the greatest magics.
I glimpsed in my mind a gleaming thought,
and a firestorm of thoughts flared in response.
I sought to raise the seed of a word,
and a bounty of words was the bright harvest.
I built with action the boon of a work,
414 and a city of works swelled around it.

In words and works my wode had grown.
More runes I found and read the staves,
as Woden did from the works he wrought;
both strong and stiff were the staves I read,
colored and stained by the crafty sage,
shaped for their deeds by the shining powers,
and carved by Hropt of the holy clan.
I heard them say of hidden secrets

423 yet to be found and the yew's dwellers
who carved and kenned those crafty runes.
To the yew without I yearned to go,
so I fared to the realms to find those runes.
At last I learned, though long my journey,
that the worlds within are the worlds without!
Seek the outside by seeking within,
once you've ordered the worlds inside.
Now I tally those nine of realms,

432 found by ashes and found by elms.
Hel is below, a hidden land
among the roots of the mighty tree.
An estate of stillness that stops all sound,
pale are its halls and pure are the shadows.
Níðhögg crawling gnaws on corpses,
releasing shades from the lyke's prison.
Thus lives before are lurking here,
records to seek for reading wyrd,

441 and Ragnarök's rune is its road to escape.
Jötunheim next is a yard of stones,
an essence unchanged though eons pass,
yet halls and homes and harrows are there.
Its venom corrodes the vital in life,

105

yet its women are sought as wives for the gods,
though the etins try to trick the Aesir.
Woden risks much for the wisdom it has,
and Hlórriði won a heart of renown
450   in a famous fight on its fimbul borders.
Svartálfheim dark is deep in the soil,
a home for the rulers of the hyde's power.
From the realms around, rivers are flowing,
channeled to forges for the choicest treasures.
Concealed from sun, it seeks to create,
but shining day makes shards of stone.
The unwary are trapped, wandering tunnels,
or slain for materials to assist its work,
459   and the serpent essence surges from it.
Vanaheim green rules vital gifts
for growth and gain and greatest fortune.
Its fields and forests are fair and bright,
and the shining shores are shadow free;
in its light the lustful may lose their way.
This home of Gullveig ere Heið she became
bears the secret of rebirth through ordeal.
Its fermentable blood is a mighty boon
468   for countering decay and caustic venom.
Midgard for Man is the middle world;
'tis a small center, seemingly infinite.
For deeds done here, the doom is greatest:
workings elsewhere have a weight that's less.
Matter may rule, but mighty spirits
can wield the gar to gainsay wyrd.
All nine meet here, all nine are fulfilled,
through birth and death in a boundless spiral,
477   ever ascending to the ultimate heights.
Niflheim cold is named for its mist,

a frigid realm with a fluid core.
In formless states, its fabrics await,
but streamed in the gap, they stiffen to ice.
Few can fathom this fortunate well
or long survive its lightless dark.
This wellspring of waters waxes in thurses,
a realm untamed with rime everywhere,
486   but a tempered drink is a treasure indeed.
Ljósálfheim bright in the lofty air
is the realm of elves who ride on the wind
among the clouds with carefree might.
This gift to Freyr is a glorious kingdom
that rhythmic breath can reach for a boon.
Fimbul Fairwheel is found through here,
and the Bifröst bridge as the bow from rain
is ridden by valkyries who render judgements
495   both up and down the ash's trunk.
Muspellsheim shines with mightiest fire;
its ever-expanding energy sparks
dissolve and destroy with zeal unmatched.
This home of Surt will harrow the ash
when the bridge is broken by his burning army.
Life cannot live in its luminous core,
though kinship it has with canting hugh.
Spilled in the gap, its sparks are useful,
504   and its tempered flood is a fimbul treasure.
Asgard is highest, the ultimate zenith,
an enclosure created for conscious main.
The heroic rule in this realm of gods
is action, energy, and always-striving:
Woden's wyrd-work for the worlds' becoming.
From here the ash can hold the gar
and with zeal can rown resounding runes.

This crown of the ash is capped by eagle,
513   the sign of ascent and soaring spirits.
The tree's tally is told at last:
realms reached by runes and their runes within.
Wide were they carved for the worlds' beings:
by Ásvið for Etins and for Aesir by Woden,
by Dvalinn for Dwarves and by Dáinn for Elves;
the path to gar was proffered to all.
At last I would add to that excellent line,
following the footsteps of famed exemplars,
522   so some myself I sang and carved.

The Tally of Skills

High were the heights of hallowed being
I reached with runes and reached with songs
and reached by roaming the realms all nine,
but more remained in the mighty quest,
for Woden issued his wisdom challenge:
Know how to write! Know how to read!
Know how to paint! Know how to pry!
Know how to ask! Know how to offer!
531   Know how to send! Know how to sacrifice!
Seemingly simple on a surface glance,
these skills run deep, their school is vast,
they lead to a triumph that truly lasts.
The time must come for testing ashes;
my time was now for a needed trial.
Through worldly work I'd wax my gar
and measure my glory by the Master's gauge.
I tell of these skills with a skaldic tally;
540   to their runes the ash is urged to rally.
Writing I know, for runic carving

and rendering thoughts with realized form,
so that words and works like water then flow.
Clear and precise are the cuts I make
with end of arm and eye of mind.
With point of gar I practice this craft
in mead for turning the tides of mind,
in wood for fixing the flow of wyrd,
549   and in stone for eternal and steadfast works.
Reading I know, to rightly seek
meaning from mystery in manifold realms:
in the lay of lots, in the light within,
in graven gar, in graves unearthed,
and in standing stones on estates of old.
From what's read I rede with right good will;
clear and precise are the counsels I give
to ash without and to oak of self.
558   Such finding of wyrd in-forms the will.
Painting I know, to power the forms
that I wrote or read with runic might,
a vivacious, vital, and vibrant main
that's a fimbul fuel for a founded work.
The pigment I use, a precious fluid,
is voice or blood or virile seed
or wode alone that waxed in my core,
with signs to seal that searing force,
567   to fix it fast on the forms to send.
Prying I know, to peer beyond
the outer realms to inner worlds,
to try and test both true and false,
to investigate all for virtues hidden:
Reyn til Rúna in rightful quest.
The seeking is key, the Self it raises,
as layers are laid in lifting the veils.

Such clarity brings occult powers,
576   and a true knowing of the Tree's secrets.
Asking I know, to earn what's Needed,
to make manifest the man within
and pour out poems in proper meter,
to surge the self through a sort of prayer.
'Tis the path to wyrd ere pitching the lots,
and hearing the hidden from the head of Mím.
Waking from slumber that sleeping woman,
the fetch within, and finding the gods
585   in their holy homes are its higher forms.
Offering I know, for altering flows
of power on pathways by pouring the bowl
to welcome wights and wondrous gods.
Through ritual wounds I can rend myself
to reconfigure my form with runes,
a gift of self that's given to Self
to gain a gild from the glory within.
The blood of beasts is the best of offerings,
594   though fraught with risk if it fails in the least.
Sending I know, to seal my works,
and speed my spells through spirit realms.
My effort projected is aimed with joy;
with force and precision it finds its way
to the inner world or outer realms.
Thus burned or buried, the boon-filled tine
to intended target will take its message.
Be certain when sending, the decision's final,
603   as the stroke of gar will go unstopped.
Sacrificing I know, for sleep at need
in the chattering mind to change its focus
and put to an end its ill opinions.
In sitting still with steady focus,

the breath is trained to benefit önd,
and the core of self is seen with clarity.
Thoughts become forms, things of substance,
to sculpt from scratch and score with gar,
612   when the light within illumines the mind.
The skills are tallied as Skilfing told,
as needful to know as the names of runes.
To pleasure and power a path they are,
declaimed by the one who kenned them first,
but another I found that's near to them;
I state this final and fimbul stave.
Succeeding I know, when the Self becoming
is hale and hearty from hallowing works,
621   and wielding the gar can gainsay wyrd.
By rowning runes and writing the staves
for wealth-gaining or winning love
or mightier goals such as Mead and Grails,
through triumph the training is tested best.
It begins and ends the graceful skills
that the Master knows and named to Man.
With nine of songs through nine of worlds
with nine of skills and the needful runes,
630   from my time on the tree, I was truly back.

The Wielding of Gar

Reborn in full with fimbul being,
in the root of my soul, the runes are seeds.
Rightly readied was my reddened gar
and I saw the truth of my seeking path.
The inner songs and outer worlds
are one fabric in wyrd's tapestry
whose warp and woof are rewoven with threads

111

fashioned and formed of the fimbul runes,
639   with gar as a shuttle that's guided by skills.
Adventure I sought, a valiant quest;
a first I found, it reformed my life.
I heard of how, in hallowed legend,
that a wyrm was crawling and wounded a man;
next Woden took nine wondrous twigs
and slew the serpent and smashed it in nine.
Two I had found to test my mettle,
a serpent without and a serpent within,
648   and soon I would see the sooth of it,
that fighting one was fighting both.
So I rowned the runes, rising in wode,
and slew the serpents with those signs of glory,
as Woden did, wielding those twigs
as a gar to hew the grave-fishes' hearts.
I sipped from the serpents their sanguine fluids
to earn the speed of eagle's speech
and conquer the fear that had kept me chained;
657   glory for gar I gained from the battle.
Adventure I sought, a valiant quest;
another I found, needful to finish.
Wielding the gar, Woden had also
sought from Freyja further secrets.
So sought Sigurd, on serpent's death,
a soaring valkyrie, Sigrdrífa hight.
For further gain I followed with gar,
and on horse I leapt the harrowing fire
666   and wrote the staves to reach my Lady,
my Rúna within and right initiatrix.
I cut the bonds that kept her asleep,
with gar like Gram against the corselet,
and that woman of wyrd then woke at last.

Her vital gifts are a varied lot,
but the power I prized was the poet's craft
and the wondrous ravens' wisdom-crowing,
to be a bearer of the burning wode;
675   from maiden I gained mead for my cup.
Adventure I sought, a valiant quest;
a third I found and throve in it.
With maiden and wisdom I made my way,
while wielding still my wondrous gar,
for a castle keep; 'tis called Montsalvat.
That hallowed hall is hard to find,
but it holds the goal that is hight the Grail!
For each the Grail is always different,
684   but the Grail for me is the Grail itself.
On the poet's path I proudly ride
for that mighty token with many forms.
Ever onward, in this endless quest,
I serve the Grail to seek the Grail
and gain in Ascent as a glorious eagle
with my Self soaring in the searing sky.
Aided by runes and through Royal Art
— a noble craft that's kept by knights —
693   I gained for my stone a great eternity.
From adventures I grow in vital being;
like Woden before, I wield the gar
to change the wyrd, to choose the slain,
and to summon the blood with searing might.
That stream of blood is steadily flowing,
and as wode it drips from my well-used gar,
to hallow the names that now I have,
to fashion a base for further quests
702   as I will to cross the wide abyss.
Giddy with might and glorious main

is the one whose work has wended this far
on the holy road of Hárr's great quest,
so remember well his mighty warnings:
unasked is better than offered too much
for always a gift seeks after gain,
and unsent is better than sacrificed too much.
Thus Woden wrote these runes for the world
711   when after it all, up he had risen.
After his time on the awesome tree,
he picked on the shore a pair of logs.
To that ash and elm he added a seed
of his own essence so they'd aim to ascend.
The gifts he gave to those goodly trees
are yours as well, so yearn for growth
and seek the Word he whispered to son,
to begin your quest for the gar's power
720   and emulate Sigtýr to own yourself.
Now Woden's work and words are spoken
from the sage's stool, sung to the trees,
useful to Men, useless to Etins.
Hale is their speaker, hale is their knower,
helped is their getter, hale are their listeners,
and told is my lay in a tally of lines
that's nine by nine by nine in full
        — the ale of power by the power of ale —
729   for the glorious work of wielding gar!

The Ascent of a Grail Knight

Invocatio

Quoth the Wode-Self, with wordhoard quickened:
"O Great Grail Maiden, bring glorious Mead
— in your cup carry the craft of Bragi —
that I sing the Work of the Word Ascent,
of the Noble Quest that quickens Knights
and how they may ride that hallowed road
to Montsalvat with valor and might,
filling their souls with Fire and Light."
And so from the Center, the source of Tradition,
010   with stead established, he streamed these lines,
the timeless tales of an eternal world,
far off, long gone, and future-coming.

The Song of the Fool

The Nameless-One pronounced these words,
the gift of beginning to go for the Grail:
"The Fool in the forest first hears the call:
by chance it came and challenged his sleep
with wondrous dreams of a wakeful life
as a noble knight when near one passed
in shining armor with shield and sword.
020   The startling vision had stirred his heart,
so he sallied forth, seeking answers.
What sooth had knights, what secret lore,
that such bold bearing beamed from their faces?
What were they like? Were they just men?
Or above all men as is Man o'er the beasts?

How were they made and hallowed with main?
Their path of power, was it proper for him?
To the lists he came, to look on their skills:
of their work and training he wanted a glimpse.
030   Gathered together, like a guild they were.
The mounted Knights were master craftsmen
in war, weapons, and wisdom's arts:
experience showed in a spiritual glow,
in constant courage, courteous manners,
and manly demeanor — a mighty sight!
The scurrying Squires were skilled journeymen,
aiding with armor, earning their keep,
learning and living this lordly trade,
and slowly but surely reshaping themselves
040   into noble knights — a needful deed!
The yeomanly Pages were young apprentices,
with a lot to learn of the lordly craft,
yet polishing armor with eager pride
and feeding horses with the finest oats,
though hard their work — a hearty start!
They jostled in jousts, yet jaunty they were;
all was in stride, even their strikings,
though hard they were hit and hurt at times.
Towards the evening, the tourney ended,
050   and the folk then gathered at a goodly feast.
At the high-seat tables, the holy Knights were.
He saw that they sat at the side of the King,
that highest Man whose hallowed being
led law and cult as the lord of both.
Of the Grail they spoke, that glorious mystery:
the talk of the town, which true knights sought
to bring back home. This best of hallows,
though hard to find and hidden well

— only the worthy could aim for its winning —
060 would ennoble heroes and renew the world
into gold again. Agog he was,
his heart inflamed by hearing mention
of that needful quest, so next he enquired
of how he might join those happy jousters.
A spark of Spirit they spotted in him,
which set him apart from the besotted rabble —
humanity's mass, the mere sleepwalkers
that lumber and dream in the light of day.
They especially aspired to expand chivalry
070 and shrewdly show its shining spirit
in a waning world. So welcome they gave
with a noble Name and a Knight's blessing
to the luck-filled lad no longer a Fool."

The Song of the Page

Proffering wisdom, the Wise-Chanter paused,
then spoke this spell of a spirit spurred:
"The Page prepared with the purest deeds;
in this guild-like group he began his Quest.
The Sword upraised was his Sign of Work,
the careful craft of a calm Foundation
080 — though one just yet he wielded not —
for he chose to defend the fount of Tradition.
To feed a horse was the first of his works.
It would always be with oats fully ripe;
though dull in form, they were deeply filling,
but corncockle, though colored brightly,
was an evil food he must ever avoid.
For care of the horse — the carnal animal —
was like care of the mind with careful inputs,

117

and so his learning was a serious labor,
090   like a strong construction's stable beginning.
First he would found a faultless base
of ready rock for raising a temple,
lest he be like the luckless man,
that brainless brute who built on sand.
Rain, wind, and flood, they ravaged that house,
and its fleeting work fell and vanished.
But Ascent was his Stone, strong and serious,
for the limitless life of a lasting work.
So lore he would learn in laying this base
100   and the culture kept by these crafty Knights,
while sharpening his mind to sharpen his sword.
In talk 'round tables, with tales and books,
he learned of ideas that illumined the realms
both far and near. First he had learned
of a proud people's perilous fall,
once like his own. The Way they had lost,
and cut they became from the craft of Truth,
and so they descended into serious errors,
yet ever thinking they were upward bound,
110   despite rejecting all spiritual heights.
The gods they replaced with glorified Man,
declaring supreme the carnal being,
wrecking the order they had rightly had,
with Man in the middle and much above.
Reason was raised, in irrational ways,
to the peak of knowing, displacing Spirit,
and the inner life they utterly devalued.
With a craft of matter, calling it science,
they looked outward for the light of Truth,
120   seeking among the sundry stars,
the earth, the air, and the ocean waters,

and by smashing atoms into smaller bits.
The world they'd count, weigh, and measure,
yet never they'd get any nearer to Truth,
bereft of wisdom that could really guide them.
Their Faustian soul, forcing outward,
conquered nature by crafting machines
to subdue the world, but their deadly trash
would waste the waters and wilderness lands,
130   and foul the air with fumes aplenty.
They waxed in war with weapons of power,
yet waned in the wisdom to wield them rightly.
Seeing mechanism and matter everywhere,
they soon saw themselves as simply machines.
Their work was reduced, for the wealth of a few,
to trivial toils unattached to craft,
degrading spirit for gains in money,
and no inner growth was opened thereby.
Their produce was banal, mere petty trinkets:
140   quantity esteemed and quality despised.
That all were equal was urged then next,
with the franchise given to the formless masses;
the ignorant ruled and the educated waned,
for their elected lords were lesser men.
Delusion it was, illusory power,
for the ruler and ruled, in reason's light,
are never the same. Thus by nasty deceit,
reigning and ruling, a right from divinity
for priests and kings, had passed to capital,
150   the hidden lord o'er the hoi polloi.
Thus Mammon sat on their modern throne,
a usurping sovereign with a scepter of lies
and an inverse crown of anti-Tradition.
Despair and anguish despoiled that folk

which fell into darkness and frivolous motion;
the once noble had wandered askew.
Phony monarchs frittered their gold
— in essence and substance, it all was wasted.
Both patrimonies and patriarchs
160   were ill-esteemed in that awful state.
Honor and Right were always besieged,
for no Chivalry shined in that shadow realm.
Men stole and killed for meaningless things.
The vulgar mass revalued all,
claiming all cultures were clearly equal,
except that some excelled in equality.
Others were lost in aimless rebellion
and so confused they followed Satan,
with zeal proclaiming an exalting lie.
170   Their culture doomed, it crashed downwards
in sick Descent to the Cycle's end.
Thus he had learned of that which was ill,
the errors to avoid and take arms against.
He heard then next of the hidden knowledge
that sustained his realm: the stone of virtue
it was laid upon. He learned of Tradition,
that higher order of the holiest values;
by its light they were led. The laity knew not,
yet it guided them well to greater things;
180   through right religion's ritual practices,
they centered on spirit and surged for its light,
aiming upwards to the ultimate source.
As a future guardian of this glorious fount
— the presence on earth of precious Spirit —
he needed to ken its knowledge consciously
and be a valiant citizen of its invisible empire.
He learned the lore of the lives of men.

A world well-ordered, working properly,
had always a place for every man,
190   and every man in his merited place.
So each had a calling for order in life,
for aiming actions to optimal goals
and providing values that varied by person,
to each his own. In the inner nature
it was rightly spotted. It was his spiritual race,
that essence within, that had urged him toward
Knighthood's calling. In Gnostic parlance,
pneumatic he was, yet made for action
and so he had sought the soldier's path,
200   mixed with monk's might. Many and diverse
were the attainment paths that triumphed for each,
where genuine craft was a joyous support
for the needful artistry of the Initiation.
Through pious devotions, priests and monks
came closer to gods, cleansing their souls.
Through bold courage, the battle-hardened
conquered themselves and came to victory.
Through focused art, farmers and smiths
changed their substances and changed themselves.
210   Unable to learn, even the laborer
could grow in soul through glad service.
He learned the lore of living cultures.
Like men they were, in their modes of life:
They had birth and growth, then glorious peak,
with decline and fall to decrepit death.
As death-doomed men had destinies within,
a culture did carry a core of wyrd
that conditioned its path and deemed its strivings.
Yet the people needed a proper order
220   to sponsor their growth: space for living,

a border to hold, a beacon of inspiration,
and a central pole for the sake of guidance.
Powerful rulers in priests and kings
were sought for keeping the citizens free
from aliens' resentment and envy of their zenith,
which would wreck their works in wasteful rage,
or the bourgeoisie's burning zealotry
for money and comfort no matter the cost,
or the mindless action of a mass unled
230   that would muddle values and mangle virtues.
A person must seek to place such order
inside his being for the best Ascent,
for the macro and micro have maxims alike.
He learned the lore of the living world,
the cycles of ages. It seemed inevitable
that from glorious peak of Golden Age
a descent to the Silver, sooner or later,
would come at last, with a cold Bronze Age
lurking behind and leading to Iron,
240   even in conditions optimal and great.
Could aught be changed to alter this course?
Could glories be kept by carefully guarding
the peak of power and prime of life?
Could the Grail give grace — grand immortality —
to a living culture as to a living man?
He learned the lore of his living self.
He waxed in knowledge of the Waters within,
that awful abyss and its icy bonds
which checked his freedom yet charged his life
250   with a fimbul force. He focused his thoughts
to find a center and to find silence.
He sought to awaken from his wakeful state,
a dreaming sleep with a deep fast grip.

He looked within to his luminous Heart,
a burning, blazing beacon of Truth,
and an inner link to awesome Spirit.
Long he had traveled, yet longer still
was the road ahead. But rightly now
he acknowledged his need for noble Questing,
260   for of path and pitfalls, the Page had learned.
So with course set, the center kenned,
and a steady heart, strengthened by joy,
he was ready to start in the Royal Art
and raise a Temple o'er his rock foundation.
With new rank proffered, the Page thus kneeled
for his rightful Ascent and then rose with dignity."

The Song of the Squire

The Wyrm-Slayer spoke, wielding a sword,
and told this tale of the task of trials:
"The Squire stood proud, with square and compass
270   to reckon his plans for the righteous Work.
As a mason builds a mighty Temple,
so should he work with the surest craft,
right proportion, correct measure,
and harmonious numbers. He made his start
with hallowed tools, the hammer and chisel,
the Signs of his Work, of serious Application.
With Fire in his Heart, he would forge more tools
of an inner nature for his outer Quests;
his steady Stone was striving's help.
280   In the art of war, he aimed to excel,
yet his proud kingdom was at peace this time,
so time it was to attack himself.
He trained with Knights as noble tutors,

123

to learn what they taught, to learn what they are.
Arms and armor was his outer Work,
one that with will waxed inner gains.
A keen mind he got through careful training
in warfare's work of wielding keen blades;
His shield of spirit shined ever stronger
290   as he surely wielded the shield he carried.
In riding a horse he rightly trained,
seeing quite well its quickening simile
for companion work with the parts of his self.
Many of virtues he made in that work,
and with the enlarging wisdom of his light within,
he kenned at this point that his careful study,
his earlier work, raised up virtues
— that still he'd develop in the striving ahead —
according to the signs of carved-runes three:
300   the Oak, the Ash, and the artful Bow.
The first was faith, full of confidence,
and a sturdy form, stalwart yet graceful,
that could sail as a ship o'er seas of danger
to survive all tests with a vigorous main,
and offering a produce, the acorns of wisdom,
that nourishes others, like the noble Oak.
The second was growth, seeking to be tall,
pushing up ever, through perseverance,
with a strong foundation and a strait discipline,
310   to be the solider that bears all attacks,
fighting fiercely to further his cause
while standing his ground, like the steadfast Ash.
The third was a course with clever thinking
and the impulse for doing, for industry's deeds,
for precision in training, to excel on his horse
and for crafting equipment and caring for it,

to be ready for war, directing his will
and aiming well, like the artful Bow.
There were more as well. For this man 'twas befit,
320   as for lords and nobles, to learn an art,
a craft of prestige, that became his station.
This one worked runes, in both wood and rock,
guiding his life with those gladsome staves,
and poems he composed, in proper meter,
arranging his soul as he arranged his words.
So through such arts, he saw the connections
in rightful works to the Royal Art,
to cultivate within a core of nobility,
an inner bearing for an outer beaming.
330   Others sought alchemy and other crafts too.
But what was truly his work and its nature,
inside the self and seen uneasily?
One squarely faced the squalls within,
in one's task of self and tests of overcoming.
Like alchemy it was, in all its phases.
Nigredo was first, a grim decomposition,
a breaking down of one's doomed being,
inside of oneself, to see as one was;
burning brought forth the black material.
340   Albedo was second, a bright purification,
wherein one washed and awakened one's soul:
the lunar light was released within;
the Waters revealed the white material.
Citrinitas was third, a triumph of Spirit,
enlightening one's life with a link to the Center:
the solar light thus seared within;
like yew's strong wood was the yellow material.
Rubedo was last, the brilliant ending
that brought one's being to the boon of wholeness,

350   gaining a glimpse of the Grail that's Holy;
most regal now was the red material.
Like rowning runes, it rightfully was.
With those stalwart signs, one started syntheses,
of ice with fire and order with chaos.
One casted lots to ken one's wyrd
and pondered the staves of one's personal realm
to make manifest the murk within,
freeing the light of one's fullest Self.
One galdored songs and engraved staves
360   to alter those lots, to create one's life,
and to slay the serpents that sapped one's Tree.
One sought mysteries in several realms —
the world within, the world without,
and the sensuous flesh — to seek the Grail.
Like three strange staves, his theurgy stood:
the Serpent, the Grave, and the searing Querth.
He trained his mind to travel within
and reach the realms, reckoned in legends,
where gods and goddesses governed wisely.
370   More mundanely, his mind developed
to ponder and value opposing views,
to seek syntheses where such were found
in third alternatives, in his thirst for gnosis.
He walked also the wooded borders,
for needful knowledge of his noble realm;
he went yet beyond the yeomen's farms
to learn of the lands that the law won't reach;
as a Serpent he wended in switching worlds.
He pondered his flesh, poor and mortal
380   learning the limits of his life and strength.
He dissected his soul, searching his traits,
to better the bright and brake the murk

that hindered his growth. With heart and trust,
he conquered fears that crippled and fettered,
lurking within. With liminal knowledge,
he wielded his will to work in the outer,
ending relations that offered no gain.
He drank a 'death' in a dire working;
while still in the flesh to strive yet onward,
390   he'd faced the Grave, that grim ending.
He focused his thoughts on fire and life,
for an inner energy to enable his rising
by burning his corpse, that body of earth
from the previous work. From a pile of ashes,
his spark of Spirit flew speedily in Ascent.
To heights he soared, to the hallowed peaks,
to breathe the pure air of primal being.
And so through Fire, the Center he reached,
merging himself with the solar essence,
400   then back he came to boost his Work.
Ever-committed to the upward path,
the Querth he'd turned to quicken his Self.
Inside the self and seen uneasily,
in all its forms his endless Work
was summed and named as Knowledge of Self.
He worked in a tradition, just one of many,
containing much Truth in tiny kernels,
to reach Tradition in the realm beyond.
So aligned with Tradition, looking to the Pole
410   and burning for gold, he began to build
an inner Imperium, reordering his person
both inside and out. By alchemy, runes
poetry, warfare, and plenty otherwise,
he won his purpose from the wellspring within,
a golden path from a Grail of sorts.

For the first of times, he truly knew,
reckoning rightly, who he really was.
But what outer boons had all become
from the arduous task and endless toil?
420   His being blossomed, with beaming face
strength in muscles, a stately bearing,
knowledge of gnosis, noble behavior,
able arguments in eloquent speech,
and a gleam in the eyes, a glorious light,
impossible to fake to the few with the sight.
In wisdom and tact he waxed greatly
for changing his style as chance demanded,
proffering always appropriate demeanor,
regardless of setting. He governed himself:
430   when among the rabble, to move carefully,
when among the Lords, to mingle and learn,
to shine with shadow or shine with light.
His pattern of doing was practiced well:
his inner work brought outer results,
for he'd linked the two through his long workings.
His sense of eternity had slowly increased:
for living each moment, though it lingered briefly,
he took the measure of the timeless realm
as a golden guide to goodly action.
440   To his excellent progress, Pages looked up,
inspired to zeal by his spiritual example,
his true commitment to the eternal Quest.
A point of turning was approached and reached;
though the Total Work was not truly finished
— it never could be while breath was needed —
much was his progress and mighty his stature.
Tried and tested, he triumphed well,
earning the esteem of those excellent Knights.

A sword he'd merited, and so it was granted,
450   but his foremost sword he had forged within,
where none could reach. So now was the time
for his sublime Ascent: a bath of purification,
a night-long vigil of needful meditation
at the castle shrine, and a call to the Sun
at bright dawn's light ere the blessed sacrament
was bestowed by the King. Then he stood proudly,
and swore the Oath, on his solemn honor
and shining sword, to shoulder the Burdens:
to defend Tradition, to fight with Honor,
460   to uphold Chivalry, and, with surest faith,
to serve the King and seek the Grail.
Outfitted with arms and armor that shined,
and readied at last for righteous Grace,
he kneeled to the King, who declared his worth
and dubbed him 'Sir' — a Solar Dignity
that confirmed his link to the luminous Pole
and set him apart from sundry mortals."

The Song of the Knight

The Grail-Servant hailed and sang the glories
of a quickening, unquenchable, unquittable Quest:
470   "The Knight rose boldly with a new red belt,
joining that company he kenned as brothers.
Having raised inside his rightful temple
and owning a link to the ultimate Temple,
he merited now the name of a Templar,
with their distinctive Cross as his stately Sign.
'Twas a great glory, for his Golden Age
had dawned within. His duty began,
as a Rider of the Realm, to roam the lands

129

and serve his Folk in the serious Work
480   with stalwart dignity — Demonstration —
being 'Sir' forsooth. And so he went forth,
mounting his horse, to manifest his name
and keep firmly fixed the fiery Gold,
that he'd won inside with work to overcome
the faults of his self — fixing o'er acceptance.
The lesser matters, he'd left behind
— the crude, vulgar, and common materials —
for the noble, refined, and numinous things,
and so he sought to excite others
490   to enjoin the majestic o'er the jaundiced mundane,
to rightly keep to the aristocratic
o'er the gaudy trash of the egalitarian.
So it was his turn to teach and aid
the Pages and Squires in their patient Work.
The crafts he kenned were the courses he taught
— runes and poetry and rightful warfare —
in the pursuit of Ascent. Outside that company,
in the towns and villages of that true kingdom,
his example inspired the zeal in others,
500   in young nobles who yearned to be,
to set forth on the path that will find the Pole
— like long ago, when he looked upon knights
as a Fool in the forest. Farther he rode,
to the yonder lands where years passed strangely
and the light of Tradition was losing its shine.
'Twas here that his Fire was a help to those Men,
among the ruins, who mourned their loss
and strove to restore a state of Grace.
Seeing him served as succor to those
510   in the hardest of places where hope was lost
— in rotten realms — who must ride the tiger.

Both gained vigor in their revolt against
a world of profanities by the welcome sight
of a Man in Ascent. But of more to his Work
there is still to tell, of his striving further.
With symbols he'd slain the serpents within,
but slay now he must a serpent without,
to establish his valor. A story of a dragon
had come to his ears. With keen boldness,
520   he sallied forth to find that serpent.
His inner work was all in truth
so this outer work had an excellent start.
The dragon had taken a damsel quite fair,
in her flower of youth and full beauty,
keeping her hostage in a hidden cave.
The high-born family of the fair maiden
lamented greatly. A mighty warrior,
a noble Knight, they'd need for her rescue,
and so came the call that he'd come to answer.
530   But that wasn't all of the wyrm's evils.
In outland realms it raided widely,
taking treasures from both town and court
to merely hoard as a heaped-up mound;
those sparks of vitality, material and spiritual,
profited none in that unneedful pile.
The people suffered by the plunderer's work;
such idled fire was an ill fortune
that caused the decline of those courts and towns.
The wyrm's foul work had wound a trail
540   of scattered wreckage. Through skillful reading
of signs and omens he sought its lair,
an accursed cave that was contra-Tradition,
and found its mouth in the foulest swamp.
Bravely, boldly, he brandished his sword

as the fearsome fiend spewed fire and brimstone.
Each had armor, enemy and Knight,
that was worn outside, but one only
was hardened within by hallowed Spirit.
The fierce, fast fighting was finished at length,
550   when the hero's steel had struck the heart
of that deadly dragon. That deed of might
would long be famed where a life of Chivalry
still stood esteemed. Astonished greatly
by the foul wyrm's fall, the fair damsel
rejoiced at once at the jouster's victory,
sorely smitten by his solar puissance.
They rode back together to the realms of Men,
returning the bulk of the treasure regained
with largesse and justice to those joyful folk
560   who now were freed from that ignoble fiend's
dastardly predation. Tradition gained
from such virtuous witness and the wise peoples'
renewed acknowledgement of noble exemplars.
His prowess grew from that powerful quest.
The damsel's family was duly impressed
by the holy hero's high-born bearing
and courteous demeanor to their comely maiden
and all folk also. With her eager consent,
the match was made and the marriage held.
570   The wise saw well, 'twas his wynnful fetch
in the form of his wife that fueled his inspiration
in pledging his jousts for her pride and honor.
His adventures continued, with valor and might.
For a time he served at the Tomb of Arcadia,
the holiest sepulcher at the heart of the realm,
in its honor guard of the most glorious Knights.
The kingdom's folk, with confidence in them,

viewed their processions of virile excellence
enjoying the pomp and justly so,
580   for that fraternity guarded a treasured heritage:
it was said to contain the secrets of gods
with the realm's first king, or if really possible,
though reckoned a myth, the mighty god
who sired that lineage. There was a secret doctrine,
to this illustrious legacy and link with Tradition,
imparted to him in perfect trust.
He was duty bound to die for that secret,
yet filled with joy by that fimbul gnosis.
Sublime and regal, it brightened his life:
590   he gained in nobility and was greatly satisfied
that the royal blood had rock-hard security.
At his service's end, he Understood much
and concurred with the words: 'Et in Arcadia Ego!'
Still seeking Ascent, and seasoned quite well,
the Superlative Quest now piqued his interest,
and so he turned to seeking the Grail!
But where could it be in a world so vast?
He started with vigil, as he started his Knighthood,
in the castle shrine with copious prayers
600   and much of time in meditations.
He considered the hallows assigned to the Grail
and said to be the signs of Knighthood:
the Cup, the Stone, and the keenest Gar.
The Cup overflowed with a curious draught,
the blood of a god that brought inspiration
or eternal life in a timeless state
or an endless bounty of every food
or drink desired. 'Twas deep with knowledge
and wisdom vast, and a woman of virtue
610   carried it forth in formal procession.

133

He had poured to others such potent inspiration
in his time as a Knight, traveling the realm.
He pondered whether he could proffer a glimpse
of eternity too or attest to a bounty
in seeking the secrets of the sign of the Cup.
The Stone stood still — establishment supreme —
shining serenely with the surest light,
the goal of the alchemists in their Greatest Work.
The phoenix rebirthed by this famed talisman,
620   but 'twas said also to send messages
by the script that appeared on its scored surface.
Steadfast he was, with a steady heart,
like a hardened rock that heroes trusted
and hadn't he heard, via hallowed runes,
meaningful messages from the mighty Center?
He regarded whether he could gain rebirth
in seeking the secrets of the sign of the Stone.
The Gar gleamed grimly with garish fire
as a potent weapon of pure sovereignty.
630   'Twas said to cause a serious bale
if wielded rashly by unworthy rabble.
It was dripping blood, and dropped were tears
when its solemn processions were seen by all.
Like the Tree of the World, it was tall and noble.
In his struggles and striving, he had stood also,
with his sovereign Self as a solar guide.
He considered his blood, brimming with soul,
and the polar power of primal Tradition
in seeking the secrets of the sign of the Gar.
640   Could the three be fused through theurgy's work
into a glorious guide to the Grail beyond?
Long in silence, he sought the light
that unified the worlds in universal gnosis,

o'er all opposites, in the essence of Spirit.
In a glorious flash, the Grail appeared
to his spiritual eyes in a splendid vision
of peace that surpassed the power of words,
yet blended with Fire and brilliant ecstasy.
Having glimpsed the Grail, his goal was now
650   to gain it fully, for the glory of many:
his King, his company, and his consecrated Self.
Since well he'd made his Work align,
part and parcel with puissant Spirit,
their boons would be all bound together.
He rode to find it, through the realms of the world,
for his vision showed the various lands
that he must cross in Quest to claim the Grail.
Long he traveled, looking everywhere,
yet worse was the world the more widely he rode.
660   In the lands out farthest that lacked all Tradition,
he questioned his Quest and queried his soul.
Could the purest Grail be the property of these?
No, it could not, but they needed it desperately.
In questing inward, in questing outward,
he realized the truth, that this relic of triumph
was surely situated in a shining center,
secure and inviolable: his kingdom's heart.
Armed with gnosis, he eagerly returned
and somehow knew the secret path,
670   both deep and dark, that went down to the vault.
He voiced the Word and the vault opened,
admitting him in to that mighty company:
the King and Lords and incomparable Knights.
He was hallowed and joined to that hidden guard
and looked upon the luminous Grail!
By his gaze on the Grail he gained a secret,

ineffable and vast, that altered him greatly.
He also knew then the earthly truth,
that in the Grail they had a glorious link
680   to the Axis Mundi: each Knight within
and by the King's blessings, the kingdom as well.
The two truths together, the Tomb and the Grail,
the effable and ineffable, were the all of his Work.
His duty to Tradition was deeply felt,
yet despite his burden, his spirit was free
and soared as an eagle. Though some would remain
as Knights after this, he knew with certainty
his task was greater, having taken well
the Ghibelline path to the Grail Mystery.
690   He knew now his duty was the needful fusion
of the regal and sacral in a realm beyond
the secure borders of his kingdom's land,
that he'd bring Tradition and the boon of the Grail
to the destitute lives living in darkness
that he saw so sorely had a serious Need.
He saw that his work had waxed in size,
becoming bigger than the company near him.
At the end of it all, in awe he realized
that he'd crossed an abyss. The King saw this,
700   and ennobled that Knight with new accolades,
raising him up to a rank of leadership."

The Song of the Lord

The Spear-Wielder spoke a spell of the work,
of the waxing of wisdom in a waning world:
"The Lord uplifted, with Light in his Heart,
then set to Work on his solar mission
to spread Spirit in Expansion's craft.

As a Lord he'd lead knights, to relight a Spark,
or with zeal preserve an exemplary Fire,
Tradition's touchstone, to dawn an Age
710   of Gold again in a ghastly realm
that had lost its link to the luminous Pole.
In full flight up, a fiery eagle
was his Sign of Ascent, and a Sword it carried,
thus showing his work in shining simplicity.
All the Ages are endless-seeming,
but Kali's Yuga is covered in darkness,
and despair floods in where Spirit is absent.
A land that was lost and living that darkness
had souls with light who had beseeched and prayed
720   to be sent a Lord from a solar company,
for harrowed and lordless, it was lacking in hope.
The call came to him via the cryptic script
that gleamed brightly on the Grail's surface.
So with Lady he left, to lead that realm,
to establish another stead of Tradition,
a secondary center of the solar puissance,
linked to the vital, living, inviolable,
and puissant Pole, the primary Center.
With trusted Knights he traveled there
730   to establish a beachhead in that stricken land
that he once had crossed in the Work of the Quest,
that the gain of the Grail be a gift to that land
which sought the Sun and Ascent anew.
A struggle he'd have to stand there as Lord:
though earnestly longed for, 'twas only by a few,
and the forces of Descent would not fold so easily.
With Sovereignty's Gar he sallied forth
to battle and reveal his burnished example.
In mere strength's main they were matched evenly,

740   yet the turtledove's force triumphed finally,
for just they alone enjoyed the boon
of spiritual armor and spiritual weapons.
Set rightfully up in that realm at last,
the Lord decreed that the craft of Chivalry
should be established and built with strength
by an Order of Knighthood that honored the Quest,
faithful to Tradition, yet formed to suit
the spirit of that land and his special knowledge.
Runes nine it taught as the road to the Grail,
750   which he learned quite well in his long questing:
the Oak, the Ash, the artful Bow,
the Serpent, the Grave, the searing Querth,
the Cup, the Stone, and the keenest Gar.
In the craft he carried, like a King he was.
Rules were laid down and rites were established;
his Order flourished, and up it Ascended
as new Knights were named (from noble stock
in all due time in that outland realm),
further securing a core of Tradition
760   to survive the onslaught of the vicious forces
of Counter-Tradition. The constant burden
of gaining ground against dissolution,
though help he had, was heavy on his shoulders,
for always the work was on the edge of change,
for failure or success in the future to come.
Yet his inner Imperium was now outer reality,
for so by his presence the searing Fire
of virile Spirit was made virtue in that land.
In the ripeness of time, there would rise a Lord
770   to set out and extend such upward striving
beyond that company as in yore he had done.
With his Lady he sired a lineage to rule,

securing the power of his puissant blood,
a formidable foundation for the physical presence
of nobility in the nation, that needful virtues
and a link to Spirit would be laid in their bones.
In time it too a Tomb would have,
a holy sepulcher and hallowed altar,
more physical founts for fortunate Ascent.
780   And so in its way, it was a Satya Yuga
that dawned in the realm for that derelict people:
sent through darkness and dread dissolution,
it passed the point of pure quantity
to right restoration by the rule of Spirit.
He remembered still the mighty realm,
the Center that sent him, and sent to it
envoys in friendship and frithful aid,
with well-ripened fruits of his further Work.
Such cordial relations and keen alliance,
790   occasionally hidden and kept in secret,
brought boons to both in their boundless Quest.
Still serving the Grail and seeking higher,
he suspected something, and explored further,
outside the center of his sacred tradition.
He Understood the upward Work
that he'd Ascended by, and saw truly
that other options would enable success.
He pondered the Cup and the powers it had,
with similar symbols in such like the cauldron,
800   along with the liquid that alighted within.
Poets it made, and a path they had,
running strange roads, for reaching Spirit.
Ascent it was not, but something different,
and that he could help in that holy Quest,
as a poet himself and proffer his Truth.

In a moment it came, the main of the Grail,
and the flash filled him with a fimbul Spirit,
the core of a system for causing Initiation,
another tradition that would ennoble Tradition.
810   Overflowing, with Inspiration
and the awe of ale, he uttered a Word!"

The Song of the Sage

The Wode-Bearer waxed in wisdom's fullness
and deemed the doom of destiny's dawning:
"The Sage in Ascent, like the Sun he arose,
glowing and strong with gallant stride,
to begin his Work in his glorious noontide,
Revelation's craft, like a right religion.
His Sign was the Sun, the Sowilo wheel
bright gleaming black with blazoned thirty-three,
820   to denote the Secret, noble and supreme.
A golden thread gambols through time,
the way to enlightenment and waxing in Spirit;
twisting, turning, it travels the ages,
in the wondrous tapestry of the world's history.
New weaves of thread the noble Sage makes,
bringing back Fire from embracing the Center,
as Prometheus brought such might from the gods.
His Fire gets form through his fimbul Word,
spoken with his Law and expounded in his Book.
830   And so this Sage, having seen to his duties
as a noble Lord, with an illustrious name
and his heir secure, out he set forth
to preach and teach his path to win
the wondrous Mead of wode-filled poetry,
and the poet's duty to pour that spirit

in powerful poems that pointed to Spirit,
so that others could taste that awe-filled state.
His task before was tiny in comparison,
for it was mouth to ear, through many contacts
840   conducted in person. His doom right now:
seeking to send forth a persistent ripple
that would inspire zeal and resound immensely,
from person to person, past those he knew
to those unseen, unmet, and unsought as well,
still yet beyond his union with death.
The woe of his work, the World to change
with one Word of Spirit, weighed him heavily,
for tall was that task, eternal perhaps,
else death alone was that doom's escape.
850   That land in which he was Lord over
looked on his teaching and allowed it a hearing,
quite readily of course. With the Cup and its draught,
many found favor, and many were filled.
His esteem grew in that gladsome state,
and many suggested that he journey not,
and stay instead. But he strode yet onward
to take his teaching for triumph elsewhere.
To a foreign land he fared then next,
proclaiming the Cup and the craft of Initiation.
860   The seed he would plant, no soil it found,
but weeds in the ground waxed there instead.
A vicious people with virulent hate,
they scoffed at his teaching with scathing words.
They Understood not and an Enemy they were,
for the secret seeds of the sacrilegious,
the corncockle of the Counter-Initiation,
had taken deep root in that terrible land.
The Sage departed — no pearls for those swine —

141

for hardened perdition is heedless of Tradition.

870 Another land that had known Ascent
and esteemed it with awe, Understood not.
Polite they were, yet they allowed it not,
his proffered message for approaching Spirit;
they turned him away, this time at least.
The Sage departed, but sorrowed not,
for well he knew that the ways were many
to reach the Grail and the realm of Spirit.
A barbarian land that had rebuked Ascent
and his erstwhile realms, he had entered next.

880 'Twas uncertain soil, yet it soon showed worth.
A reception they gave to his serious message;
where seeds before had sickened and died,
a sprout sprang forth, and Spirit was established.
They rose then up in righteous virtues
through the lengthy work of waxing in Light.
The wise ones there then worked for peace,
building bridges and bringing accord
between their people and the people of Ascent.
They'd been brothers once, now brothers again:

890 no more brother wars! At such brilliant work
the Sage then smiled, for the circle of Tradition
was well widened by such wondrous receptions;
in the rotting realms, rare were such wins.
By Message and Work, he'd remade the world.
To his original home he rode again,
to share his Message with the shining company
that had set him forth on Ascent's path.
No scorn nor scoffing, but askance some looked,
especially the Fools and the sprightly Pages,

900 for they Understood not. The eager Squires,
they sought and questioned: some were quickened,

but some were confused. The same Word heard
the wise Knights and Lords, by wisdom illumined;
they gleaned the gold threads of great Tradition
that ran through his Truth, threading the tapestry
of the world for better, for waxing Spirit.
They honored him well for his excellent Work.
exalting him higher for his zeal and success.
Yet an end to all will always come,
910 though long it takes for that last day's arrival.
When long had passed, for a last of times
in advancing age, his valor was tested.
An Enemy assaulted that excellent kingdom;
those fierce foemen fought to destroy
that land of Light and its link to the Center.
For King and Tradition his courage still waxed
and he took to the fight. Triumph was had
by that glorious company of the Grail's keepers,
but the Sage was slain with sword in hand."

The Song of the Saint

920 The Glory-Eagle galdored utterly,
in a state established as a stellar stone:
"The Saint Ascended, unseen by the living,
like a soaring eagle in a sun-filled sky
with valor and might, from his Montsalvat
in that earthly kingdom, to the awe-filled mystery,
that yearned-for realm beyond the world
the Montsalvat of vital main,
in the heavenly kingdom for a holy embrace
of the Great Mystery, glorious Rûna.
930 With the Grail attained, his Great Work now
was the endless task: Immortality.

143

Behind was his corpse, with his holy blood
fully poured out, the final proof
that without and within, ever to the Grail,
that holiest hallow, he'd held his faith.
He'd unflinchingly served, to the final moment,
his King and Quest and the craft of Chivalry.
And so in his honor, a solemn funeral
was arranged for him in the realm at its heart.
940   He was placed on pyre in proper ceremony,
with the Raiðo rune as Rûna's symbol
upon his breast. With pouring tears,
many of the folk were mourning his loss.
They burned his body with brilliant Fire,
as a symbol of sending his soul to Spirit.
They interred his ashes by the Tomb of Arcadia,
in the Hall of Heroes with those Holy Knights
who stayed steadfast to the stone-cold end,
defending and advancing the force of Tradition.
950   But was he truly gone, with return impossible?
Some doubted his death and deemed that he lived,
saying his soul still soared in their skies,
saying his spirit still inspired the faithful.
Mighty miracles were made in his name,
or was it his glory that galdored from beyond,
showing his will must surely survive?
Some others said his Self was reborn
in the world again for his Work to continue,
perhaps in grandchildren of his high-born offspring
960   or a noble lineage of Knights from the Grail.
But where truly was his wondrous spirit?
Could its realm be reached, rightly ere death?
But dead to the world that one might be,
and the lands might then be lost to him.

The Wise will ever wonder such things
as they seek Ascent for their Self's profit.
The Saint had lived the Seeker's life;
further he'll seek in the formless realms
— beyond all gnosis and beyond all knowledge
970 of life and death — for the limitless All
with noble speed as a Knight of the Grail."

Exvocatio

Quoth the Wode-Self, with wordhoard quenched:
"Hale is the hearer and hale is the singer,
for Ascent's way has been said through words,
welcome to the Wise, wondrous to the Fool,
and profit to the presence of potent Spirit;
open is this way for the earnest seeker.
That Knight Ascended, and by Need shall I,
as these winsome words work their magic."
980 And so from the Center, the source of Tradition,
he gained the Grail by the gladsome Mead
and the timeless Runes of the eternal world
that's far off, long gone, and future-coming.

Initiatory Sumbel Toasts

Óðrœrir (January 2011)

Hail to Bölverk
who burrowed fast
as a sneaking snake through rock.
In lust for mead
he laid with Gunnlöð;
for three of nights he knew her.
He deeply drank
those draughts all three;
that potent mead he pilfered.
Hail to Arnhöfði,
to Asgard he flew,
taking that mightiest mead.
For the gods he won
glorious Óðrœrir,
and for skalds and scholars alike.
For that precious find
— a fimbul gift —
hail to ominous Óðinn!

Hail to the praise-makers
plying their songs,
Egill and Eyvind and more.
Hail to the poets
of priceless verse,
Refur and Bragi and the rest.
Hail to the pourers
of precious mead,
hail to the poets of our people!

Hail to my quest,
for heartily I seek
Óðrœrir, the foremost ferment,
Óðrœrir, the mightiest mead.
So that like Woden I win
the wode-stirring draught,
as Bölverk burrowing to Gunnlöð,
as Arnhöfði flying to Asgard.
So that like poets of the past
I pour out the mead,
as Egill and Eyvind and others,
as Refur and Bragi and the rest.
For greatest becoming
and glorious refrain,
hail to the Mightiest Mead,
hail to my holiest quest!

Disting (February 2011)

Hail to Rindarson,
hail to Óðinsson,
the avenger of brightest Baldur.
Grown but a winter,
he gained revenge
and quickly requited that death.
No hands he washed,
nor hair he combed,
before that deed was done.
Baldur's slayer
he bore to the pyre.
Hail to valiant Váli!

Hail to Refur;
he wrought revenge
for the grievous insults given.
By careful thought
and clever plans,
he slew that slandering family.
Hail the coal-biter
and crafty poet;
hail to roguish Refur!

Hail to my workings,
weighty in might,
with many of speeches to speak,
with many of Runes to rist.
I work to write,
resolute in purpose,
for much of mead to gain,
for much of mead to pour.
Such deeds of doom,
undaunted I perform,
like Váli avenging Baldur,
like Refur wreaking revenge.
I avenge forthrightly
my forebears' conversion.
Hail to my duty to tradition,
hail to my highest of quests!

Walburga (April 2011)

Hail to Óðinn,
hail to Freyja,
welcome Walburga to sumbel!
Drighten of dread,

the darkness is past,
and the light of the Lady we've reached.
Waning is Máni,
waxing is Sunna,
and Walburga is faring forth.
Ward this stead
and steer us well;
hail to gods and goddesses!

Hail to Egill,
a hero of Óðinn
and a wise and powerful poet!
Hail to Óttar,
a hero of Freyja
who hallowed her harrow with blood.
Poetry and blood,
power they give:
gain through words and works.
For trust in might
and trust in main,
hail to Egill and Óttar!

Hail to my blending
of bright and murk,
of darkness and light in my life,
of subjective and objective in my life.
I travel the roots
and travel the branches,
as Egill and Óttar did once,
as Óðinn and Freyja do always.
The synthesis I seek,
its substances I praise:
holy is the fiercest Fire,

holy is the awesome Ice!
With Sunna and Máni,
I surge in might,
Hail to Mysteries and Mead!
Hail to my holiest quest!

Heroes (May 2011)

Hail to Gaut,
god of heroes;
he speeds them toward their wyrd.
Hail to Ygg
who hung on the Tree;
the rede of the Runes he got.
Hail to Bölverk
who brought the Mead;
powerful poets it makes.
To the god of heroes
who is a hero himself:
Hail to ancient Óðinn!

To Hengest and Horsa
who harried Britain:
they seized that land for Saxons.
To Sigurd and Beowulf,
for slaying dragons,
that bravest and boldest of deeds.
To Egill and Refur
who authored poems:
they poured the mightiest mead.
To numerous awesome
others unnamed:
their deeds and doings we toast.

They trusted in might
and trusted in main,
great were their words and works.
For glorious doom
and greatest deeds,
hail to the heroes of the Folk!

Hail to my doom,
the deeds of a hero,
seeking the rede of the runes,
seeking the power of poetry.
I aim to do
as Óðinn did:
hanging on the highest tree,
winning the mightiest mead.
I do with heart
as heroes did:
completing worthy works,
writing powerful poetry.
With glorious might
and glorious main,
hail to my holy strivings,
hail to my hero's quest!

Runes (July 2011)

Hail Óðinn,
oldest of gods,
for his nights all nine on the tree.
Bread and horn,
both he lacked,
during that long ordeal.
The might and main

of mysteries he won
by giving self to Self.
For those runes he took
and told to Man,
hail to excellent Óðinn!

Hail to the Gilds
of the Holy Runes
that seek the mighty mysteries.
Hail the elder
of ancient days
that left the staves in stone.
Hail the modern
of here and now
that furthers those forms anew.
For the glorious main
of greatest mysteries,
hail to the holy Gilds!

Hail to the Runes,
those holy mysteries
and awesome Óðinn who taught them,
and the great good Gild that keeps them!
The might and main
of those mysteries I seek
to follow Óðinn's footsteps,
to join the Gild in joy.
I quicken my quest
by quaffing the Mead
and pouring that potion like Óðinn
and risting my runes like Masters.
For the Gild and its god
and the greatness I seek,

hail to the holy Runes,
hail to my highest goals!

Mímir's Well (November 2011)

Hail to Mímir
of the holy well;
its water he wards and drinks.
Under Yew's root,
in Jötunheim,
from Gjallarhorn he gets that drink.
Óðinn gave
an eye for a draught,
the price of wisdom's power.
For keeping well
his cosmic duty,
hail to mighty Mímir!

Hail the scholars
and skalds of old
for mustering memory's draught
to keep the lore
alive and well
for its bright rebirth in our time.
In our work today
that wealth we use
for the glory of gods and men;
for the needful layers
they laid in the well,
hail to those famous folk!

For starting the path
with powerful drink,

following the road of Runers,
following the road to Fellow,
I boast my Naming;
now I'm a Learner,
yet forward I look in my life,
yet forward I seek to my Self.

The Drighten's doom,
draughts from the wells:
I work to that distant wyrd,
I will to surpass that wyrd.
For success in my goals
and the glory I seek,
hail to my quickening quest,
hail to the holy Rune-Gild!

Óðrœrir (January 2012)

Hail Óðinn,
the holy eagle
and sneaky serpent as well.
He sought that sumbel
— from Suttung he took —
in his quickening quest for wode.
He won that bounty
— the best of gods —
for skalds and scholars alike.
For pouring out
precious Óðrœrir,
hail to awesome Óðinn!

Hail the word-smiths
who waxed with mead

154

and left us the lore in poems!
Hail the researchers
who sought the mysteries
to understand those staves!
Through the bounty of both
has Bölverk's drink
returned to Midgard's Men.
For pouring out
precious Óðrœrir,
hail to the skalds and scholars!

Hail to my quest
for the holy mead —
I work to emulate Óðinn,
I work as skald and scholar.
To follow his path,
I ponder mysteries:
the runes of the sneaky serpent,
the runes of the awesome eagle.
In being a skald
and scholar as well,
I craft with wode my words,
I craft with care my words.
For pouring out
precious Óðrœrir,
hail to my skaldcraft and scholarship,
hail to my quickening quest!

Birthday (December 2012 Version)

Hail to Óðinn,
Yggdrasil's rider,
whose road to runes I follow.

Hail to Bölverk
who bears the mead
that I seek to win myself.
For showing the sure
and shining path
of heroes though hard it be,
which I in wisdom
willingly follow,
hail to all-wise Óðinn!

Hail Bragi,
husband of Iðunn,
for his shining staves and stanzas.
He sired skaldcraft,
this son of Óðinn.
Hail to brilliant Bragi!

Hail Víðarr,
Hropt's avenger
and enemy of the evil wolf.
For strong silence
and a step that's sure,
hail to valiant Víðarr!

Hail Eirík
Hlaðir's Jarl,
and Eirík the Red from Iceland,
the Norse heroes
I'm named after.
Hail to the awesome Eiríkar!

Hail Egill,
Icelandic skald,
and Bragi Boddason the Old;

their word-smithing
I work to surpass.
Hail to these skillful skalds!

To thirty-six years,
yearning for greatness,
but with my path and purpose found,
and with the best and brightest to come.
I will my way
toward my glory
by working the wyrd of Runes
and working the wyrd of Mead.
The path of scholar
and the path of skald:
I seek them each for success,
I blend them both for greatness.
For a life of works
and wynnful living,
hail to my Work of the Words,
hail to my birth and being!

Yule (December 2013 Version, Revised)

Hail to Jólnir,
the Yuletide's lord,
for the blessings bright we've gained.
Yare this year make
as we yearn for glory.
Hail to Jólnir for Yule!

Hail to Woden,
wisdom's drighten,
and lord of wode and wynn.

For mastery of Runes
and Mead and Grails,
hail to wonderful Woden!

Hail the Erulians
of elder times:
those mighty masters of Runes.
For the carvings in stone
that kept the tradition,
hail to those awesome Erulians!

Hail the Skalds
who were skilled with words:
those excellent masters of Mead.
For the wode they won
through their works of verse,
hail to those skillful Skalds!

Hail the Knights
of the noble Quest:
those glorious masters of Grails.
For the spiritual growth
they inspire today,
hail to those noble Knights!

Hail this year past
of harvests great:
I won and rowned the Runes,
I poured and made the Mead,
I sought and gained the Grails!
The glories ahead
are greater still:
passing tests with triumphs
and gaining great becoming.

My will is strengthened
for the way to come,
to spin the yarn of the year
that yare the year is made.
I ride for the glory
of Runes, Mead, and Grails!
Hail to the yielded year,
hail to the year ahead!

Learner-Naming Boast (November 2011)

Eirik traveled
to Texas for Moot,
sealing in ceremony
the sought-for goal,
and with draught from horn
was deemed a Learner,
to Master ᚱᛁᛋᛏᚾᛏᛁ
rightfully pledged.

At last I'm Named
a Learner of the Gild,
to follow the road of Runers,
to follow the road to Fellow.
Hail the Master!
Hail the Learner!
Hail to the bettering of both!
Hail to the Holy Rune-Gild!

Fellow-Naming Boast (February 2013)

Always onward,
I aim to advance.

With joy I've joined
the journeyman's ranks,
for on Disting's Day
I was deemed a Fellow
in the mighty Rune-Gild
by Master ᚱᛁᛋᛏᚾᛏᛁ.

Finally Named
a Fellow of the Gild
I ride the road ahead,
I ride the road to Master.
Hail the Master!
Hail the Fellow!
Hail to the bettering of both!
Hail to the Holy Rune-Gild!

Master-Naming Boast (August 2016)

In Ascent I've succeeded
and soared to new heights.
On Midsummer's Eve,
Master ᚱᛁᛋᛏᚾᛏᛁ
ruled it rightly
with runes of might,
that I'd made it so,
that I've a Master's substance.

Next by Naming
at that noted Thing,
power in person
was passed through rite
and I took my place
in that distinguished company

of the Gild's Masters,
with galdor and mead.

Hail the Masters!
Hail the Mastery!
Hail to the bettering of both!
Hail to the Holy Rune-Gild!

For the Doors (December 2013, Revised)

This ale I raise
to the end of Nine Doors
and its great and wondrous gains.
This stout I raise
to the start of the New Path
and its mighty road to mastery.
Hail to the needful Nine Doors!
Hail to the needful New Path!

Personal Boast 1 (June 2011)

Hail to my living
and lengthy history:
thirty-four years of youth,
thirty-four years of thought.
The best are ahead,
brightly shining,
seeking success and fortune,
reaching runes and mead.
I honor my gods
and ancestors great
with glorious deeds and doings,
with worthy words and poems.

Sure as Sunna,
shining and bright,
hail to my happy wyrd,
hail to my happy life!

Personal Boast 2 (August 2011)

To my troth and trust
in my trying quest,
and the keenest courage of Týr,
and the keenest customs of Folk.
The hand was forfeit
but the fiend is bound:
I wax from the weal of sacrifice,
I build on the base of tradition.
A Thing without,
a Thing within:
right is the order outside,
right is the order inside.
For the customs to keep
and the courage to do,
hail to sacrifice and siður,
hail to my holy work!

Yule Resolution 2010 (Regular Dróttkvætt)

Rightly riding sought I
Runes and mighty boons and
now wakeful in will by
Wode-Stirrer's great spurring,
for Yew this year now my
yearning will thus burn with

bids for drighten's deeds and
dreams of roles and goals great.

Yule Resolution 2011 (Iambic Dróttkvætt)

My wode and wynn from mead,
toward research it's poured;
with greater deeds I greet
the glory yet in store.
As scholar-skald in Gild,
with skill my doom I fill,
and yare I make the year
at Yule to brightly rule.

Yule Resolution 2012 (Modified Dróttkvætt)

Beer-might I, Wode-Bearer,
bring to the world, singing
galdor great and writing
glory staves and pouring.
I'll with skill as scholar
to Scandi-realm grandly
in just, joyous questing
journey thus for learning.

Yule Resolution 2013 (Iambic Dróttkvætt)

For rightful wins and Runes,
I'll ride and seek in pride.
I'll make with wode my Mead;
its might and flair I'll share.
Great spells I'll work with Grails

and grow my light as knight.
In me they're forged and merged,
those mains from three of gains.

Mead-Work Poems

The Óðrœrir Working

Weary of the war,
the Wanes and Ases
spat together their spittle,
shaped Kvasir in a kettle.
Wisest of wights,
he wandered throughout
worlds to give his wisdom,
realms to give his rede.

Dwarves so greedy,
Galar and Fjalar,
wasted that noble wight,
butchered that noble being.
His blood they mixed
and brewed with honey:
Óðrœrir, the potent poetry,
Óðrœrir, the mightiest mead.

Galar and Fjalar,
they foolishly slew
witless Gilling and his wife,
the sire of Suttung and his wife.
They bought atonement
from the tide that threatened
by surrendering the mead to Suttung,
by handing it over to Hnitbjörg.

As Bölverk into Hnitbjörg,
I burrowed to Gunnlöð:

165

three of nights I knew her,
three of draughts I drank.
As Arnhöfði I flew
to Asgard from the depths,
taking the potent poetry,
taking the mightiest mead.

Craftily won
and keenly used:
the power and poetry of Óðrœrir,
the bounty of Boðn and Són.
The mead is held
in holy steads:
the wisest are waxing in might,
the drightens are drinking in joy.

Now to pour
this potent brew
in the craft of wode and will,
in the craft of skald and scholar,
I will my way,
that work I live:
pouring the mightiest mead,
pouring awesome Óðrœrir!

Three Draughts from the Vine

I heard of a path
to heightened knowing
sparked by a special vine:
that the eye-opening
Ayahuasca brew
could change your life with its light.

I sought with respect
— receptive and reverent —
to gain its gifts of spirit.
At first I thought
to find a way
to unity, health, and heart.

The first of draughts
had flickered briefly
but little of light I saw.
The second of draughts
was a serious dud,
though I purged a mighty puke.

On another night
I had another try
with faith in the medicine's magic.
The third of draughts
was a thrilling trip;
the change I'd chosen to seek.

Its spirit came
and spurted through me,
bringing vibrant visions.
I purged with voice
a puking of demons
and saw the lights unseen.

But I'd drunk from that cup
the death of my ego;
both mind and memory departed.
Left alone
I lurched adrift
and feared my physical death.

Reduced to nothing,
a dead man walking,
yet still I struggled for life.
Bit by bit,
reborn I was,
in Midgard remanifested.

With life anew
from a look at death,
my work in the world goes on,
for I took a spark,
returned from darkness,
for my unity, health, and heart.

The Way of Old Words (Revival of Alliterative Verse)

The ancient verses,
their elder forms,
I seek to raise
and rightly sing.
Though dead for long,
life I will give
and breath and being
back to the staves.

First to their graves,
I go to find them.
Spells to raise them,
I rightly speak.
The draugur staves
stand and walk;
spells they speak
to spur my work.

Wisdom they give;
I gift in exchange.
I honor their graves;
in awe I stand.
I depart to use
the power I've won
in further questing
to quicken the forms.

I seek the Mysteries,
their might I need.
I hang on that holy
and highest of trees
to win the Runes
and rightly use
their power in quest
for poetry's Mead.

I seek the Mead,
its main I need.
A mountain I reach,
rightly in quest.
The maid within
I meet in tryst;
by knowing that woman
I win the Mead.

By Runes and Mead,
ready I'm made.
I bid the dwarves
bodies to shape
and staves to stand
for sturdy words;

verses I write
with vigor and might.

I galdor runes
to give them breath
and pour the mead
to make their blood.
With the gifts they live
gladly anew:
skaldic verses
skillfully wrought.

The Mead Working

Wōðanaz, Wiljōn,
Wīhaz: in thy names!
A home for my hidge,
a hall I lift!
I first forgive
for failures myself,
then to might and main
I commend myself.

For holy fire
I follow Woden;
breath of fire
is breathed on self.
Rising flame
and rising ghost
are by valknut bright
bound with might.

Everlasting is birth
and life and death —
the holy work
of the highest three.
The mother of Runes
and her mighty children:
their mysteries I seek,
many and subtle.

Mighty Wōðanaz,
wisest of gods,
my ghost to thy might
and main I give.
The Word throughout
the world I send:
Reyn til Rúna,
rightly it goes.

Wisdom is won,
by will it is taken.
Mother Earth,
my might she watches.
Blood of wisdom,
water of blessings:
the mighty mead
with main is loaded.

Hail all the Ases,
hail all the Wanes!
Helm of Heaven,
hail to Woden!
Earl of the Earth
— Ice and Fire —

hail the holy
and highest three.

Indwelling in mead
is mighty wisdom;
in my ghost and lich
it lives forever.
The work is wrought;
its wisdom and craft
works in my soul
and the souls of Runers.

Rune-Work Poems

Poetic Translation of the Original Rúnatal

For nights all nine,
I know that I hung
on that wyrd and windy tree,
by gar wounded
and given to Óðinn,
myself to myself I gave,
on that mammoth tree
of which Man knows not
from where the roots do run.

Blessed with no bread,
nor brimming horn,
down below I looked;
Runes I took up,
roaring I took them,
then back unbound I fell.

With mighty songs nine
from that much-famed son
of Bestla's father Bölþorn,
a draught I drank
of the dearest mead,
from the Stirrer of Poetry poured.

Then fertile I became
and full of wisdom,
and I grew and greatly thrived.
A word got a word
by a word for me;

a work got a work
by a work for me.

Runes you will find
and readable staves
— very strong those staves,
very sturdy those staves —
which were painted by the powerful speaker
and made by the magical advisors
and risted by the invisible advisor.

For the Aesir 'twas Óðinn,
but for Elves 'twas Dáinn,
and Dvalinn for dwarven kin,
and Ásvið for etin kin;
I risted some myself.

Know how to rist!
Know how to read!
Know how to paint!
Know how to pry!
Know how to ask!
Know how to offer!
Know how to send!
Know how to sacrifice!

Unasked is better
than offered too much;
always a gift seeks gain.
Unsent is better
than sacrificed too much;
so risted Thund
ere the rule of Man,

where up he rose
and after came back.

New Old Norwegian Rune Poem

Fee is the family's row;
forest will make wolves grow.

Slag is from ill iron;
oft will deer on snow turn.

Thurs causes women's woes;
winsome are few from throes.

Outlet is faring's fate;
free from sheath, sword seeks bait.

Riding is rough on steeds;
Reginn forged sword of deeds.

Sore is curse to a kid;
caused pale, the evil did.

Hail is the coldest corn;
Kjalarr shaped world new born.

Need makes a narrowed pick;
nudes in frost will freeze quick.

Ice we call a broad bridge;
blind men need some steerage.

Harvest is human gain;
hate did Fróði his grain.

Sun is the light of land;
let holy deemings stand.

Tyr is a one-hand wight;
work the bellows aright.

Birch is a limb, leaf-green;
Loki's deceits were keen.

Man is Midgard's equip;
mighty is the hawk's grip.

Water is force as fall;
fine gold's cost is quite tall.

Yew is winter green wood;
when burned, it scorches good.

New Old Icelandic Rune Poem

Fee is a family's row
and the flood-tide's beacon
and a boulevard for the barrow-fish.

Drizzle is clouds' weeping
and a cutter of ice-rims
and to herdsmen a hated fiend.

Thurs is ill for women
and an alpine dweller
and the groom of Guarding-Rune.

Ose is ancient Gaut
and Asgard's chieftain
and the lord of Valhalla's legions.

Riding is sitting's bliss
and a swift journey
and hard on the mounted horse.

Sore is a curse to kids
and a cost of scourging
and the residence of rotten flesh.

Hail is a frozen grain
and a forceful sleet
and a shot of sickness to snakes.

Need is a bondmaid's throes
and a burdensome condition
and toilsome weather for work.

Ice is a river's rind
and a roof of waves
and death to a man who's doomed.

Harvest is gain for men
and a good summer
and a full-grown field of crops.

Sun is the shield of the clouds
and a shining glory
and an endless sorrow to ice.

Tyr is the one-handed god
and the wolf's leavings
and a sovereign of sacred shrines.

Birch is a leafy branch
and a little tree
and a wonder of youthful wood.

Man is man's delight
and Midgard's product
and oft an ornament on ships.

Water is a roiling river
and a roomy kettle
and the rightful field of fish.

Yew is a bending bow
and a brittle iron
and oft to arrows a striker.

New Old English Rune Poem

Money is a benefit to men everywhere
and ever must each offer it freely
to gain good doom from a gracious drighten.

Aurochs is strong-willed and extremely horned;
the beast will battle, bravely with horns.
This famous moor-stalker is a fierce creature!

Thorn is very sharp to thanes everywhere,
harmful to grasp and harsh immensely
to every human who hangs among them.

Ose is the origin of all that is speech,
to wisdom a support, to wizards a comfort,
and to lords everywhere a delight and joy.

Riding is easy in the athelings' hall,
but very strenuous to the striving one
who mounts a horse over miles of road.

Torch is fiery, notorious to the quick,
bright and shining, burning oftest
on the inside for athelings at rest.

Gift is for men a grace and praise,
an honor and support; to all wretches,
those without else, it is alms and survival.

Joy is not lacked if little are woes,
sores, and sorrows, and the self has bliss,
fair prosperity, and fortified dwellings.

Hail is the whitest of wheats; it whirls from heaven's height,
it wends on gusts of wind, and it goes to water thereafter.

Need is narrow on hearts, though humans can name it help,
often even salvation, if early enough it's valued.

Ice is frigid and ultra slippery;
it glistens like glass or a gorgeous jewel;
'tis a frost-made floor, fair to behold.

Harvest is glee, when a god allows,
a lord of heaven, the land to provide
radiant fruits for the rich and poor.

Yew is a rood that's rough outside;
firm in the earth, it is fire's keeper,
a joy on estates, and sustained by roots.

Perth is always play and laughter
where warriors sit, with the wise and the proud,
in the hall at mead, happily together.

Elk-sedge has a home, oftest in marsh,
growing in water; it wounds grievously,
burning with blood the bold warriors,
the doughty ones, who dare to grasp it.

Sun is to seamen a source of hope
when faring over the fishes' bath
till the brine-stallion brings them to land.

Tir is a token; troth it keeps well
with athelings all and 'tis always on course,
over night's darkness, never betraying.

Birch is fruitless, but bears nonetheless
seedless branches and beautiful twigs.
With a lofty crown, delightfully adorned,
it is tall and leafy, touching the sky.

Steed is for earls an atheling's joy,
a hoof-proud horse, when heroes together,
nobles on chargers, exchange their speech;
'tis a remedy always for restless men.

Man is cherished in mirth by his clan;
yet everyone betrays the others eventually,

for his doom is deemed by the drighten's will:
the tattered corpse is entrusted to earth.

Sea is for men seemingly endless
if they venture out on a vessel that's tossed,
and the fierce billows frighten them greatly,
and the brine-stallion rebukes the reins.

Ing was seen first by the Eastern Danes,
among all men, till he moseyed back.
O'er the waves he went, and a wagon followed;
the Heardings named that hero thus.

Estate is for men extremely dear,
if they oft enjoy in their own dwellings
a rich good life, right and seemly.

Day is from drighten and dear to men
as the measurer's light; it is mirth and hope
to the haves and have-nots and a help to all.

Oak is on earth an aid to men
as a food for flesh, though it fares often
o'er the gannet's bath; the great sea tests
if oak timbers have an atheling's faith.

Ash is very tall and valued by men;
it holds its stead with a strong foundation,
though many a man will move against it.

Bow is for earls, and athelings too,
an honor and joy; 'tis excellent on a horse
and gear for war, welcome on a journey.

Serpent is a stream-fish, but still it enjoys
its food on land; it has fair dwellings,
surrounded by water, and a winsome life.

Grave is loathsome to lords everywhere,
when inexorably, the awful flesh,
the cooling corpse, comes to the earth
as a horrid bride — harvests wither,
pleasures falter, pledges shatter.

Querth is a quern and it quickens fire;
it burns the tree, the bier-doomed thane,
and it frees the soul to seek the heavens.

Cup is well-known by keen wode-bearers
as the holy horn, heavy with poetry,
essential at sumbel; this sail of dwarves,
a way-gain of Woden, is a winsome grail.

Stone is strongest as a stead-blessing
if hallowed with writing, with heathen runes:
'tis ever an altar; this etin's heart,
a life-giving sign, is a lasting grail.

Gar is sovereignty, a sorcerer of war-woods:
it changes the wyrd, it chooses the slain,
it summons the blood; this brand of Woden,
enormously mighty, is a noble grail.

Short Rune-Tally

Fehu the Fee
is the fire of life.

Uruz the Aurochs
is the awful beast.
Þurisaz the Thorn
is the threat of danger.
Ansuz the Ancestor
is the awesome god.

Raiðo the Wagon
is the rightful toil.
Kenaz the Torch
is the crafty fire.
Gebo the Gift
is the giving exchange.
Wunjo the Joy
is the wonderful blessing.

Hagalaz the Hail
is the hardest trial.
Nauðiz the Need
is the narrow resistance.
Isa the Ice
is the arctic land.
Jera the Year
is the yearned-for harvest.

Æhwaz the Yew
is the evergreen wood.
Perþro the Piece
is the play with lots.
Algiz the Swan
is the awesome valkyrie.
Sowilo the Sun
is the sought-for stone.

Tiwaz the God
is the trothful one.
Berkano the Birch
is the barren tree.
Ehwaz the Horse
is the excellent partner.
Mannaz the Man
is the middle being.

Laguz the Lake
is the liquid deep.
Iŋwaz the Hero
is the earthly lord.
Dagaz the Day
is the dearest of lights.
Opala the Legacy
is the ancestors' gift.

Moderate Rune-Tally

Fehu the Fee
is the fire of life;
both strife and strength
stem from that gold.
Drightens deal it
for a doom that's best;
thus wyrms and wolves
are warded off.

Uruz the Aurochs
is the awful beast
whose horns give wyrd
to that holy well.

The brave and bold
have the best of lives
when fighting and feasting
as fierce as that beast.

Þurisaz the Thorn
is the threat of danger:
a harrowing harm
that hinders life.
That force is used
for defense as well,
though it runs the risk
of ruin when grasped.

Ansuz the Ancestor
is the awesome god:
the master of wode
whose might is in words.
Wizards' wisdom
and warriors' struggles
are the twin domains
of this twilight lord.

Raiðo the Wagon
is the rightful toil
of the holy horse
in hale ritual.
If wheels and axles
are well maintained,
the road's rhythm
is readily heard.

Kenaz the Torch
is the crafty fire

that is set to serve
the self's intent.
'Tis a dire scourge
— dreadful to bairns —
that causes cankers
if care is lacking.

Gebo the Gift
is the giving exchange
between a two
who have taken frith.
Both back and forth
it binds together
the liege to his lord
and life to the gods.

Wunjo the Joy
is the wonderful blessing
of fellows in frith
feasting together.
Sores and sorrows
are safely managed
if the boon is blended
with brightest wisdom.

Hagalaz the Hail
is the hardest trial
to unwary ones
who are walloped hard.
It turns to water,
but if taken quickly
and planted well,
it is precious corn.

Nauðiz the Need
is the narrow resistance
that cuts against
the careful plan.
If struggled against,
strength it will make;
if heeded well,
help it will bring.

Isa the Ice
is the arctic land
that roofs and stills
the roiling waves.
'Tis folly for fey men,
famously gleaming,
but when frozen fast,
'tis a fortunate bridge.

Jera the Year
is the yearned-for harvest;
for grinding gold
'tis the greatest cycle.
Proper planning
and prudent rest
can avoid the vice
of the vicious mill.

Æhwaz the Yew
is the evergreen wood;
'tis a link to life
and living through death.
Outside and in,
Yggdrasil is real,

and fire is found
in its fimbul roots.

Perþro the Piece
is the play with lots
and the spirited speech
spoken in sumbel.
The web and well
are wended through
and boldly faced
by bravest thanes.

Algiz the Swan
is the awesome valkyrie
who brings to Gaut
the best of Goths.
The horn of the hart,
like that hall above,
is pride and power
and purest spirit.

Sowilo the Sun
is the sought-for stone
and a shining wheel
in the sure seeker.
This shield of clouds
will show the way
to the one who works
for wisdom's gain.

Tiwaz the God
is the trothful one;
with craft his courage
secured the wolf.

188

Both firm and fast,
his famous token
is a glowing guide
in the grim darkness.

Berkano the Birch
is the barren tree
that is brightly loaded
with beams and leaves.
'Tis birth and being
and breaking the seed;
this mother makes
the moments of life.

Ehwaz the Horse
is the excellent partner;
for riding the realms
he is rightly called.
The two together
are truest friends;
their tearing apart
is a terrible end.

Mannaz the Man
is the middle being;
for the work and wyrd
of worlds he's needed.
To birth and death
his being is doomed;
heroes have harnessed
this hidden wisdom.

Laguz the Lake
is the liquid deep;

both whales and waves
wax there like leeks.
Gold from the drink
is gained through work,
but serpents guard
the sea's treasures.

Iŋwaz the Hero
is the earthly lord;
o'er the wave he came
and then wandered back.
The wending wain
worked its magic:
an oak was grown
from the acorn's grave.

Dagaz the Day
is the dearest of lights;
'tis seen in Measurer
yet sent by Drighten.
Paradox power
and pure twilight
will work one's wode
to awakened heights.

Oþala the Legacy
is the ancestors' gift:
the strong estate
with stone for walls.
Customs carried
across the years
are precious treasures
in a potent tribe.

Rúnagaldraljóð

As Wode-Bearer,
with will I speak
to inspire the self with song.
I rown the Runes
and rede them well,
a song of sayings without
as galdor for going within.

Fehu the Fee
is the fire of life —
that gold is strife and strength.
Deal it well
for a doom that's best:
to many that force should flow
and within that fire will flame.

Uruz the Aurochs
is the awful beast
whose horns give wyrd to the well.
Seek the power
of primal forms
that lurk and live in wilds
to light and lift the self.

Þurisaz the Thorn
is the threat of danger,
a sharp and harrowing harm.
Treat with care
that tricky etin
to save your skin from scrape
and save your spirit from spoil.

Ansuz the Ancestor
is the awesome god
and master of word and wode.
Journey along
his joyous path
in the world and gain your goals,
in the self and seek your runes.

Raiðo the Wagon
is the rightful toil
of the loyal and helpful horse.
Work to maintain
the wheels and axles
of your ride in the world all-wide
for your ride through realms unseen.

Kenaz the Torch
is the crafty fire
that is rightly set to serve.
Burn it bright
— being careful —
to forge your life with lust
and forge your spirit with spells.

Gebo the Gift
is the giving exchange
of two between themselves.
Give and take
with greatest wisdom
to honor your friends and folk
and honor your self and soul.

Wunjo the Joy
is the wonderful blessing

and work of fellows in frith.
Blend with wisdom
this bounty for weal
to grow in grith with friends
and among your souls inside.

Hagalaz the Hail
is the hardest trial
and grain of coldest corn.
Weather well
this world of storms,
and tend your seeds outside
to wax a Word within.

Nauðiz the Need
is the narrow resistance
upon your plans and goals.
Strive against it,
starting a fire,
to keep the cold away
and build your might and main.

Isa the Ice
is the arctic land:
it is hard against your growth.
Work in wisdom
with winter's force
to bring a rightful rest
and clear a clouded mind.

Jera the Year
is the yearned-for harvest
and cycle for grinding gold.
Properly plant

with patient work
to reap the world's rewards
and grow the gains of spirit.

Æhwaz the Yew
is the evergreen wood
and a link to life and death.
Study it well
and strive for its fire
to wax in lore of worlds
and surge in lore of self.

Perþro the Piece
is the play with lots
and sumbel's spirited speech.
Learn the layers
and live with wode
to win through rightful risk
and die with soaring soul.

Algiz the Swan
is the awesome valkyrie
and a link to glorious gods.
Raise your gaze
to the rainbow bridge
and in nature know the gods
so in spirit you'll greet the gods.

Sowilo the Sun
is the sought-for stone
and the sailor's guide and grace.
Mind that wheel
when wandering around

to keep in the world your way
and keep in your life that light.

Tiwaz the God
is the trothful one
whose courage secured the wolf.
Carve his name
and call on him twice
for victory in war and work
and victory in self and soul.

Berkano the Birch
is the barren tree
that is bright with limbs and leaves.
Water it well
to wax in being
and become a force in fact
to become a might with main.

Ehwaz the Horse
is the excellent partner
and best for riding through realms.
Honor him well
and always keep him
for blessings and boons in life
and help and health in spirit.

Mannaz the Man
is the middle being,
vital to the work of worlds.
Grow the gifts
given by Óðinn
for honor from kith and kin
and glory from heroes and gods.

Laguz the Lake
is the liquid deep
and land of whales and waves.
Search that dark
and seek its gold
to master the might of seas
and master the main of souls.

Iŋwaz the Hero
is the earthly lord
who over the wave then went.
Go out, come back,
and grow in between
to change your worldly wyrd
and change your spark of spirit.

Dagaz the Day
is the dearest of lights
by Drighten sourced and sent.
Mightily seek
its mirth and hope
to work awake with light
and soar aware with wode.

Oþala the Legacy
is the ancestors' gift,
the strong estate with walls.
Graciously guard
this greatest treasure
to preserve your kindred clan
and the trust of tribal spirit.

Rûna the Mystery
is the rightful source

of the runes we name and know.
Ever and always
with effort seek her
in worlds all-wide without,
in worlds all-wide within,
and in forms of flesh between.

I've sung complete
a song of mysteries
and poured it through might of mead.
Deeply drink
this draught of runes
to alter with ale your Self
and alter with ale the World.

The Yggdrasill Working

Yggdrasill, Yggdrasill,
Yggdrasill I call,
and self to Self
I sing with speech!
I truly stand —
a stately tree;
the awesome sound,
the ash I sing.

Peering down,
darkness lifting,
the runes I scry,
screaming fiercely!
The words I speak
are a wisdom spell;

from word to word
by word I go.

From work to work
by work I go,
then Fuþark, Fuþark,
Fuþark I call.
I rist the runes
and redden them well;
the fimbul staves
are filled with might.

The runes I found,
the runes I took,
the holy runes
I rightly name!
Four and twenty
are the twigs of blood;
strong are the staves
I stain in self.

The Rûna Working

Rûna, Rûna,
Rûna I call,
and *Reyn til Rúna*
I rist with speech.
The fire is kindled,
into the flame I gaze;
the mystery I see
sinks into my being.

Food of self
I seared for Rûna,
holy drink
I drank to Rûna,
holy food
I fed to Rûna —
to Rûna within
and Rûna without.

Rûna thrives
in three of steads:
Rûna dwells
deep in the world;
Rûna sings
in my self and mind;
Rûna flares
in my flesh and blood.

Rûna I love,
Rûna I seek;
I call to Rûna,
come into my soul,
and come as flesh
in the form of a lover.
Hear my words,
heed my words.

The Full Moon Working

Our Máni bright
is a mighty sight;
we hail tonight
his holy light.

Greatly shining,
sure in being,
fiercely singing,
firm our seeking.

Runers hail him,
right and holy,
the Moon of Helgi,
the Moon of Sigurd.
For the living folk,
firm is that link,
strong and mighty,
to mainful ancestors.

The wood in the fire
is food for the Moon;
the blazing needles
nourish his might.
The dright of runers
readily obtains
a gift for this gift:
a glad exchange.

Hale and joyful
from Hati's jaws,
Máni comes
merrily again.
We wend our way
with winsome minds;
his might and main
we meet in full.

To the living dright
dear are the moons;

twelve in all
and twelve we call.
We learn their lore,
in their light we're born,
and merrily mead
to the moons we drink.

Máni, Máni,
Máni we sing!
Our moods are made
mighty indeed,
and great is the main
for mind we get.
Again the moon
has met his height!

Grail-Work Poems

The Grail Triad

Calc is a cup, a keen chalice
of dearest drink that dazzles the mind.
It spurs the spirit of speech in sumbel,
so fast will flow a fountain of words:
the pouring of poetry, a powerful gift.
The essence of Self, seek it within;
fill your being to the brim with life,
overflow in fullness with fimbul runes.
This cup is a grail, gleaming with craft.

Stan is a stone, a steady rock,
a firm footing, and fast it holds.
Upon a pile you pour your mead
in glad giving to gods and wights
for bright blessings in blóts you hold.
Carve on with care the keenest of runes
for eternal works teeming with might,
or to honor ancestors with awesome main.
This stone is a grail, great and stable.

Gar is a spear, a great weapon,
but greatest is Gungnir, when grimly cast.
It hallows the host to Hangatýr given
and the awesome Einherjar in afterlife chosen
from the battle-dead who bravely fought.
Destiny's power is deemed from its point;
to Grímnir's runes 'tis a gateway road;

be weapon wounded if Walhall you seek.
This spear is a grail, glorious in spirit.

Querth (Grail Slam Prelude)

The Querth is zeroth; it quickens zeal,
that potent spark that surpasses fire.
A Grail it is not, but a gateway to them
is found by turning this flame-maker,
a queer sort of quern whose quarry is dross,
grinding out fire like grain to flour.
Its friction-formed flame, fierce and holy,
is as passion for gold of the purest kind.
But what is best to burn with its work?
The lore will lead, that link to Tradition,
and surely show the Should of the matter,
for fire makes flesh the fodder of gods.
Hallowed kine keep their kindreds whole;
the beef binds boons borne from the gods.
The ash offering of the atheling's corpse
will send his soul in Ascent to the gods.
For an ancient hero of elder days,
fire made his flesh the food of an eagle
when Prometheus stole for Man that spark.
For the deed he lost his liver daily,
for defying Zeus in furthering us.
Did you do well with your deal of that gift,
or does your spark grow dim with neglect?
What need you to know for the next of steps?
Heed the Tokens for turning your Querth,
for fire as well is found in the Grails:
the curious lift of the Cup's elixir,
the staves flickering on the Stone's surface,

and the gleaming torch at the Gar's apex.
For kenning its rune, the key is this:
Solar glory is seen in fire,
an earthly hold of that heavenly orb
and fount which changes form and substance.
Don't seek the path of psycho vandals
who burn churches in blind rages.
The essential fire must be set within
to burn your soul with a brilliant light.
When such fire is fixed, firmly within,
then can you quest on the quickening path
as one of the worthy who may win the Grails
through inner fire and alchemy's Work,
detaching yourself from the trite substance,
humid and base, of the human flesh,
to regenerate with joyous arising
in Solar triumph and eternal Ascent.

Cup (Grail Slam Part 1)

The Cup is first, that famous chalice.
Was it the one with wine from a god
in Thirty-Three at Thursday Supper?
Did Jesus drink of, then drop in his blood
in destined death on the day after?
Or is it inverted cup of vaginal flesh,
the womb of Mary that waxed with his seed,
bearing an heir with blood that's royal?
So many forms for this magical fount
have been proposed to bridge the mystery.
More I will say to mark the prospects.
Is it Dagda's Cauldron that dealt out food,
so that all who came could eat their fill?

The secret Soma that sated Indra,
gifting him strength and giving him life?
The many memories in Mímir's Well,
where an eye obtains all its wisdom?
The horn of mead with holy poetry
that's offered out by Óðinn alone?
Not for the masses is this needful magic;
the elite alone can look for a drink.
Its liquid provides a link to Spirit;
its nectar ennobles the knight in his quests.
A transcendent source of soul's support,
'tis a potent essence of purest life,
for Ascent is seen in a single drink,
along with a glimpse of the longed-for center,
of Mighty Valhöll or Montsalvat,
of Mount Meru or mystic Arcadia.
But seek you must, if Ascent you'll have,
for this Grail gives not if you give no effort.
A hint we have, from its hallowed traditions,
for always by lady, in all the stories,
forth it's carried in formal procession.
So look to your Lady to learn the secrets
of this Lunar Grail whose liquid gift
is the prized elixir and the promise of alchemy.
Then seek and succeed if your soul is worthy,
and dare a deep draught of the drink it holds
for creative sparks of inspiring awe,
the treasure of knowledge that tempted Faust,
and the urge to action that ale can raise.
From the masses that move in a mindless daze,
its power will set your soul apart,
and onto the path of all becoming.

Stone (Grail Slam Part 2)

The Stone is second, that sacred rock.
Was it the heavy lid of a hallowed tomb
that rolled away from a risen god?
Or Lapsit Exillis from Lucifer's crown,
a star-born stone that strikes the soul
with light prolonging the life it touches.
No less are the forms that lead the way
to this mystery's heart, which may be a heart.
Wolfram's tale told of the tidings it gave
through briefly visible brilliant letters.
But the Head of Mímir holds such tidings,
though spoken by a spirit bespelled by charms.
The Lia Fail, it fiercely roared
to proclaim truly the King at Tara;
the Grail gave also goodly notice
of the lords and ladies who'd lead its order.
But how to quest for this hallowed rock?
Consider a symbol, sent from above,
that great green glass, a gift from the sky:
the jewel of Moldau. A joining it shows,
of fire from the air to an earthly form,
of a gift from the gods to a growth of nature,
alike to the way that living wood
was changed to human by a choice of the gods.
Consider Parzival, that proud simpleton
who grew to become the greatest of knights,
completing his quest with compassionate heart.
But what of the hearts of heroes and warriors,
like haughty Hrungnir and Högni the Bold?
The former was stone and formed a valknut;
it stands for the courage of the steady heart,

shown by the latter, unshaken on platter.
Such hearts make worthy and hallow a knight
to seek Montsalvat and this Solar Grail,
a glorious jewel that gleams like the sun.
To all the others, I can only say:
begone for concealed are the secrets of gods.
I offer last a lead from alchemy,
that sacred science which sought to perfect
the basest metals to brilliant splendor.
Know in your heart the needful truth
that your Self is the metal which must Ascend,
and as with alchemists, ever you'll say:
"This greatest Stone is the Goal of our Work,"
and reach the stead of rock-solid being.

Gar (Grail Slam Part 3)

The Gar is third, that glorious spear.
Was it the lance that gored a god in the heart,
its wielder holding the whole world's fate?
Surely it was, but are you sure of the god?
Christ at Calvary, cut by Longinus,
is only one of the wonders to seek.
Look to the North for a likelier fit.
Offered on Yggdrasil, Óðinn was hung,
gored by a gar but given to Self,
and he grasped the runes that govern fate.
Other weapons will offer their wisdom:
the lance of Lugh, alight with fire,
kept quenched in water to cool its tip,
and the sword of Sigurd that slew a dragon,
reforged from the pieces of a former sword
that broke in battle on a brandished spear

which was Óðinn's own, the awesome Gungnir.
But mysteries remain, marked by the stories.
Why does it bleed, and then water rain
from the eyes of all who onto it look,
when forth it's carried in formal procession?
The bold true knight will be tested greatly
on the quest to claim and carry this weapon.
But what shall I say to the unworthy seeker?
Do not take it, terrible sinner!
For your daring folly, a dolorous stroke
will damn your world with a doom of ill.
An elite only, with a link to Self,
can wield this force for reworking fate,
for the gar is like that glorious pole
honored ever as the Axis Mundi,
the transcendent center and source of Spirit.
'Tis the sovereign power seen in a king
and shown to all through his shining scepter.
If true you are, to triumph in quest,
your higher self must handle the shaft
and point with power this Polar Grail.
Then think fierce thoughts to thread the fabric
in the holy weave of the hidden web
and rule with runes the run of the world.
'Tis all 'bout Óðinn, to act as he does,
a sovereign self in a sundered world.
In this final token, you'll find the truth
of Thirty-Three and theurgy's work
for gaining eternal and glorious action.

Ask the Question

I sought the Center, I sought adventure;
I sought for growth and gain for my soul.
I sought the Grail and I sought for a hof
to hallow as home for higher learning.
The work of wyrd: a way it found
to fuse them both in a fateful blend
and to shape my Should and show me a sign
to remake my fate with mythic forms.
For the old enclosure, I aimed the gar;
the spell would speed, spurring me on
to do what's needed and dare for more
and after anguish to Ask the Question.
First came waiting, then came terror;
the lesser offer alighted first.
By gar I was wounded, by gar I was healed.
Would I seek safety and accept the edge?
Or risk it all and roll the dice
to seek the center that I sought the most?
A fire of discord filled my being
— an awful ache then owned my gut —
and I laid the lots to learn my wyrd.
The cast was clear, my course was set:
I'd choose this chance to challenge fear.
I released the hope of the lesser offer
and fully committed to my first of choices.
By gar I was wounded, by gar I was healed.
My being was bent, my brain was trapped
with no peace for thoughts in this place of qualms.
Yet I felt alive, and the fire lingered,
pushing me on as I passed the days.
The tension was pressed to talking out

and then action-taking to end the crisis.
Over-polite I've always been,
but on seventh day I sought an answer
from Ultima Thule and Asked the Question,
the certain fate of a seeker undaunted.
By gar I was wounded, by gar I was healed.
The grant came quick, the grail of my hof,
and dark desolation, though dire, was lifted,
waxing the healing of my wounded heart.
To Thule I came with thanks in my soul
and claimed the stead I secured by action,
hallowing my home as a heathen temple.
My hof was Hof; 'twas hight truly,
and rightly in it I wrote this poem,
the one that I gained through way of the Grail.
In a Montsalvat I made this verse
as I strive to live the Stone's lesson
and keep to the quests that quicken my life.
What is the way? Its work is simple:
'tis ever and always to Ask the Question.

Charms and Invocations

Waking Stave

This dawning day
brings deeds of might
for us the bold and brave.
Awake today,
aware I'll live,
and find a Rune to rown,
and find a Rune to write!

Washing Stave

In thy seed and blood
and searing might,
myself I wash through will,
O great Gaut,
glorious lord
and fimbul father of all.

I wash away
the will of ill
that dwelled within and out.
Off it runs
like ice that's struck
by the great and golden sow.

Away ill will,
away with evil
out with all bad health.
Between my eyes

is the Ægishjálmur:
all evil it stemmed and stopped
as through me its power poured!

Food Stave

This fine food
be filled with power,
with awesome might and main.
Excellent energy
to enable my work
flows and fills my being,
lights and lifts my being.

Drink Stave

I deeply drink
this draught of might
filled with force of life.
Bright blessings
from brimming cups
give help and heart to my work,
give boost and boon to my will.

Mead Stave

This heathen spirit
of honey I drink
to stir my wode and will.
With mead I mix
the magic of skalds;
I live the work of wode.

Stave Coloring Stave

The staves are stained —
strong is this magic,
carved and colored
with crafty mind.

Sleeping Stave

I wend my way
into the well of sleep
to thee O wynnful Woden.
To learn thy ways,
I'll listen well,
finding runes to read,
and seeking wode to win.

Mead Loading

O Mainful Mead
of Midgard's realm,
be filled with the fimbul spirit
that the Drighten of Darkness
drank from Óðrœrir,
that our words are spoken with will,
that our words are spoken with wode!

Alu Invocation

ᚠ   Ale of Óðinn in overflow I gained,
ᚱ   that powerful Liquid Leek
ᚾ   that raised my Urox energy.

Fuþark Invocation

ᚠ The flowing Fire of Fee within
ᚢ ordered my Urox power
ᚦ for Thunder against the Thurses
ᚨ through Aesir's Ale and Oaken fettle
ᚱ to rightly Ride the worlds
ᚲ with kindled Torch of craft.

Meðuz Invocation

ᛗ With mighty Mead I made inside
ᛗ of energy from awesome Fetch,
ᛞ the dearest Day has dawned within
ᚢ and given fimbul Form
ᛇ to a living Link with gods.

Wōþuz Invocation

ᚹ Wynn has caused my wode to flow
ᛟ from base of Odal awe
ᚦ as thrusting Thorn of thrilling power
ᚢ and raised the Urox energy
ᛇ to Valkyries' zone of zeal.

Norse Solar Invocation

Great All-shining, you are Everglow,
the Fair-Wheel and famed Sky Fire;
as mighty Sunna, send me your main,
and fill my life with your light
to speed my spirited soul!

214

Heart Fire Invocation

O flickering Fire,
enflame my Heart
and kindle its spark of Spirit!
Let it burn and blaze
as a beacon of truth
and a pyre of power within!

Querth Invocation

The Querth I turn to quicken my fire
filling my soul with fimbul main:
it burns the dross that burdens me,
and it burns my being to embolden me!
Through fire I soar, free to ascend,
to gain the Grails in glorious Quest!
O Querth, Querth, Querth, quicken me now!
O Querth, Querth, Querth, quicken me now!
O Querth, Querth, Querth, quicken me now!

Cup Invocation

From Cup I drink to call down wode
and wax in wisdom from well of memory.
This lunar grail is my Lady's gift
with the godly drink of great becoming.
Its flowing force fills my being,
urging my soul to aim for Ascent.
O Cup, Cup, Cup, give craft to me now!
O Cup, Cup, Cup, give craft to me now!
O Cup, Cup, Cup, give craft to me now!

Stone Invocation

By Stone I live with strongest heart
and hear of things that are hidden from all.
This solar grail is the self's high goal,
the godly rock of greatest being.
This sign of Ascent is sought by Knights
and truly obtained through trial and quest.
O Stone, Stone, Stone, make steady my heart!
O Stone, Stone, Stone, make steady my heart!
O Stone, Stone, Stone, make steady my heart!

Gar Invocation

With Gar I deem to govern wyrd
and gain renown through glorious deeds.
This polar grail is the peak of main
that's wielded well for worthy action.
With Ascent in the soul, 'tis the seeker's joy
and the way from words to works of legend.
O Gar, Gar, Gar, make great my Work!
O Gar, Gar, Gar, make great my Work!
O Gar, Gar, Gar, make great my Work!

Grail Maiden Pledge

O Great Grail Maiden, my Glorious Lady,
I pledge my Sword and service to you.
My deeds today I deem your gift;
with thoughts of you I thunder forth.
I boldly brave my battles for you;
I attain in trust my triumphs for you.

One-Liners

"Hammer give might and the heart of a knight!"
"Hammer make healthy and whole myself!"
"O star-born stone, make stellar my heart!"
"By will I wot that worked it be!"

Eagle Invocation

May the fire and the force
of the fimbul eagle
be with my soaring soul!

Staves for the Self

Introduction
Strong and stout
are the staves I have
to chant when change is required.
I rowned and risted
the runes with will;
I name the charms I know.

Against Useless Actions, ᚲ·ᚺ
I know a first
for fits at random
if I wander aimless in work:
the power to steer
of Perth and Sun
turned me to glorious goals.

For Cheerfulness, ᚲ·ᛈ
I know another

of needful use
if sour sorrow threatens:
I played with Perth
and pondered Wynn;
this charm had cheered my mood.

For Inspiration, ᚠ·ᛄ
I know a third,
a thirst it quenches
when making mead is needful:
I harked to Óðinn
and hailed the Yew;
my wode was strongly stirred.

For Concentration, ᛁ
I know a fourth
to foster will
when focus of mind falters:
to counter the chaos
I called on Ice;
my concentration returned.

Against Inaction, ᚦ·ᛏ
I know a fifth
to fight a blight
if in stillness fast I'm stuck:
the Thorn's power
and threat of Need
had spurred my spirit to act.

Against Fear and Paranoia, ᛗ·ᚠ
I know a sixth
for a certain trouble
when fears are flooding my mind:

I remembered the might
of Men and Aesir;
that flood was drained and dried.

For Good Health, ᚠ·ᚾ·ᛚ
I know a seventh
as a soothing balm
if health and wholeness falter:
I focused on Leek
and Fire and Aurochs;
my vigor and wellness waxed.

To Focus on Goals and Honors, ᛋ·ᛏ
I know an eighth
to add to my fire
if goals seem dark and dim:
I sought success
through Sun and Týr;
my yearning brightly burned.

To Increase Intellectual Production, ᛃ·ᚲ
I know a ninth
for needed increase
if flow of mind falters:
the power of Year
and prod of Torch
restored the stream of craft.

To Increase Charisma, ᚲ
I know a tenth
to top off my sparkle
when among people I mingle:
I called on Torch

to keep my being
raised with charisma bright.

To Increase Communication, ᚹ·ᚷ·ᛗ

I know an eleventh
to lift my talk's dearth
if to Elm or Ash I speak:
with help of Gift
and Human Joy
my words were wise and free.

Against Hesitation and Delay, ᛏ·ᚺ

I know a twelfth
to tweak my motion
if stuck when struggle is chosen:
I trusted in Týr
and tried with Hail;
effortless action followed.

For Good Sleeping at Night, ᛜ·ᛒ

I know a thirteenth
to think of at night
when day is done at last:
through Ing I slept
and also by Birch;
rested and ready I waked.

For Wakefulness and Awareness, ᚠ·ᛗ·ᛇ·ᛋ

I know a fourteenth
fortunate to have
to grow and gain in wits:
by Óðinn and Day
and Elk and Sun,
awake and aware I lived.

To Increase Perseverance, ᛏ·ᛇ
I know a fifteenth
to firmly stand
when troubles and trials are lurking:
through might of Týr
and main of Yew
I persevered with vigor.

For Speed in All Things, ᚱ·ᛖ
I know a sixteenth
for swiftness sure
if a spell of speed is needed:
I Rode on Horse
and raced with haste;
my actions all were fast.

For Skill in Tongues, ᛃ·ᛏ·ᚨ
I know a seventeenth
to assist my studies
when training in the tongues of the Folk:
Óðinn and Year
I uttered with Týr;
my skill with words was waxed.

For Improving the Will, ᛇ·ᛋ·ᛁ
I know an eighteenth
to elevate my will,
when purpose and power are needed:
I sang the Yew
with Sun and Ice;
steady and strong it had been.

For Gain from Exercise and Stretching, ᚾ·ᚢ·ᛇ
I know a nineteenth

that's needed by lich
when exercise I seek:
with Need I uttered
Aurochs and Yew;
in strength and stretch I gained.

For Wise Decisions, ᛉ·ᚨ

I know a twentieth,
I trust it well
if I need to pick a path:
Elk and Óðinn
I uttered for wisdom;
of choices I chose the best.

For Needful Money, ᚠ

I know a twenty-first,
a treasure to have
if much of money I need:
A Fee I formulated
for fortune great;
the funds then flowed to me.

For Strengthening the Enclosure of Self, ᛟ

I know a twenty-second
that's timely to sing
when my self is stressed and strained:
my bequest of Odal
I called to mind;
my borders bolstered fast.

For Awakening the Fetch, ᛉ·ᛗ·ᛞ

I know a twenty-third
— in the twilight used —
when I strive to stir my fetch:

Elk and Horse
I uttered with Day;
my valkyrie was waked through will.

For Obtaining a Lover, X·‹
I know a twenty-fourth
to turn a woman
when her pleasure and play I want:
Gift and Torch
I galdored for tryst;
we'd gone together to bed.

Conclusion
Mind well these songs
and sing their might;
they're useful if used at need.
Be hale by hearing,
whole in knowing,
and live your life through will.

For Self-Actualization, ‡
A final I know
fulfills the rest —
for might and main it's best.
I hearkened always
to the Hail inside
and sought my Self with pride.

Workings and Blessings

An Óðrœrir Working

1 — Opening
[Perform a suitable hallowing, then sit before the stall or table with three cups, each with one mouthful of holy liquid in it.]

2 — Hearing the Words
Speak the word *Óðrœrir* nine times, listening to your own voice each time. Then speak the word *Boðn* nine times, followed by *Són* nine times. [As you complete each word, envision its respective cup illuminated by a mystical light.] Then repeat the formula *Drekktu djúpt inn dýra mjöð* three times, again listening attentively to your own voice. Then speak the formula *Vinndu af verkum inn verðuga mjöð* three times, followed by *Austu æ inum æzta miði* three times.

3 — History
[Recite stanzas 1–3 of "The Óðrœrir Working," which is in the Mead-Work Poems chapter.]

4 — Drinking
[Recite stanza 4a of "The Óðrœrir Working."]
[Drink from the three vessels in one gulp each.]

5 — Flight
[Recite stanza 4b of "The Óðrœrir Working."]
[Stand erect, and in a single exhalation, intone æ-u-i-o-e-a. While doing so, envision a bright force rising up from the depths through your feet, genitals, solar plexus, throat, and finally reaching the top of your head. Perform this intonation a total of three times.]

224

6 — Fulfillment
[Recite stanza 5 of "The Óðrœrir Working."]

7 — Thinking
[Sit and silently think of the idea of Óðrœrir — and the presence of this substance in the universe, now flowing through your blood and mind.]

8 — Closing
[Recite stanza 6 of "The Óðrœrir Working."]

An Yggdrasill Working

Harrow Setup: 24 individual rune lots, or a single stave with the entire Fuþark, and something to write or carve the Fuþark on and with.

1 — Opening
[Stand before the stall in the Isa staða. Place a complete set of 24 individual rune lots at your feet, or alternatively, a single stave carved with the entire Elder Fuþark. Perform the Hammer-Signing.]

2 — Hearing the Word
Speak the word *Yggdrasill* nine times, listening to your own voice each time. Then repeat the formula: *Gefðu sjálf sjálfum þér* three times, again listening attentively to your own voice.

3 — The Hanging
[Face North. Stand in the Æhwaz staða and sound the æ-vowel on nine exhalations. During this time, strongly envision yourself hanging on the world tree as Óðinn did. After the ninth exhalation, look down at the runes at your feet and scream.]

4 — Fulfillment 1
[Switch to the Isa staða and face forward. Recite *Hávamál* 138–141 in Old Norse or Modern English.]

5 — Enacting the Runes
[Switch to sitting at the harrow.]
Speak the word *Fuþark* nine times, listening to your own voice each time. Then repeat the formula: *Ríst Rúnarnar* three times, again listening attentively to your own voice.
[Then, on a piece of paper, write the entire Fuþark in order, concentrating on imbuing the power of each rune into the stave forms. Alternatively, carve the Fuþark in a piece of wood instead.]

6 — Fulfillment 2
[Switch to the Isa staða and face forward. Recite *Hávamál* 142–143 in Old Norse or Modern English.]

7 — Call to the Runes
[Switch to the Elhaz staða and look up. Call out the rune names, one ætt per breath.]

> "The Runes I found, the Runes I took,
> those Runes I rightly name:

Fehu-Uruz-Þurisaz-Ansuz-Raiðo-Kenaz-Gebo-Wunjo
Hagalaz-Nauðiz-Isa-Jera-Æhwaz-Perþro-Elhaz-Sowilo
Tiwaz-Berkano-Ehwaz-Mannaz-Laguz-Iŋwaz-Dagaz-Oþala."

8 — Thinking
[Switch to the Isa staða, face forward and silently think on the staves of the Elder Fuþark.]

9 — Closing
[Recite *Hávamál* 144–145 in Old Norse or Modern English.]

An Óðrœrir Blessing

Altar Setup: Horn, Vessel, Bough, Bowl, Spear, Óðinn Idol.
Speaker Setup: Cloak, Eye Patch, Valknut.

1 — Spear Warding
The speaker walks the perimeter with a spear three times while
saying:

> "This gar guards now
> our garth tonight
> for the power prepared
> and poured from Óðrœrir."

Then when finished he says:

> "By might and main
> we're meetly warded,
> against the ways
> and wights unholy."

2 — Reading
The speaker recites the poem "Mead Quest" by Eirik Westcoat.
[For the poem, see Eirik's *Viking Poetry for Heathen Rites*.]

3 — Rede
The speaker recites the following to the gathered folk:

> "Remember tonight
> the might of Kvasir:
> The wisest of wights,
> wisdom he gave,
> till greedily slain
> by Galar and Fjalar;

Óðrœrir from his blood
was brewed with honey."

"Its winning by Óðinn
we honor tonight;
through mighty craft
that mead he got.
He favors the few
with flashes of wode;
skalds and scholars
are skilled by the drink."

4 — Calling
The speaker makes the following calls in the first three lines of
each half stanza, while the gathered folk respond with the
fourth line of each half stanza:

"Hail to Sváfnir,
you slithered to Gunnlöð!
Crafty serpent,
we send thee welcome!
Hail to Arnhöfði,
to Asgard you flew!
Soaring eagle,
we send thee welcome!"

"Hail to Bölverk,
the bale you worked
secured that sumbel;
we send thee welcome!
Hail to Óðinn,
you honor the skalds
with sweetest draught;
we send thee welcome!"

228

5 — Loading
The speaker then returns to a position in front of the harrow, pours the mead into the drinking horn, and holds it aloft, saying:

> "Our deeds and doings
> we deem as gifts;
> our might and main
> with mead is blended.
> A gift for a gift
> is given anew:
> the power of poetry
> poured as Óðrœrir."

6 — Drinking
The speaker makes the sign of the valknut over the horn and drinks. He hands the horn to each true individual with the words:

> "Awesome is this mead;
> Óðrœrir it is called.
> Drink now deeply
> this draught of skalds."

As each true man or woman is handed the horn, he or she makes the sign of the valknut over its rim before drinking. The remainder of the horn is poured into the blessing bowl.

7 — Blessing
The speaker touches the mead in the blessing bowl with the tip of the spear while saying:

> "This holy mead
> I hallow to Óðinn,
> to honor his quest

for quickening Óðrœrir.
His struggle we celebrate;
we strive ourselves
to garner that gain
by growing in worth."

The speaker now takes up the evergreen bough and sprinkles the Óðinn idol saying:

"Hallowed be Óðinn,
the highest of gods!"

Next, he sprinkles the harrow, saying:

"This harrow I hallow
with holy mead."

The speaker then sprinkles all true folk present, saying to each one:

"With brightest mead
I bless you now —
awesome Óðrœrir
and Óðinn's power."

8 — Giving

The speaker then returns to the harrow and takes up the blessing bowl, carrying it to a point just east of the harrow. There the mead is poured out with the words:

"To you, Óðinn,
we offer today;
take well the gifts
we gladly exchange."

9 — Leaving

> "Hail to Óðinn,
> the highest of gods,
> for the wode and wynn
> and wisdom we gained.
> Our work has here
> for weal been wrought;
> we go forth now
> in glorious moods."

Grail Mysteries Ritual

0 — Altar Setup
Fire, Cup, Stone, Spear. Incense is optional. If there are enough participants, a procession of the Grail Hallows may be added.

1 — Fire Warding
The speaker walks the perimeter with fire three times. When finished he says:

> "The fire of Querth now fiercely wards
> this hallowed stead for our holy work:
> for the power prepared and poured from Cup,
> for the life and love that lurks in Stone,
> for the deeds and doings that we deem through Gar."

2 — Recitation of the Lore
"Let the lore of the Grail Runes be spoken."
The speaker then recites Eirik's Old English Rune Poem stanzas for Cweorð, Calc, Stān, and Gār in Old and New English. [*They are in this volume: the Old English is in the Runes for the Grails chapter, and the New English is in the Rune-Work Poems chapter.*]

3 — Presentation of the Grails

The speaker holds up the Grail Chalice and says:

> "This chalice is sought by champions everywhere;
> a bounty it brings, brimming with main,
> and your soul will soar with a single draught."

The speaker holds up the Grail Stone and says:

> "This strongest stone is the steadfast heart;
> right rede it renders through runic methods,
> and if life is lacked, life it will bring."

The speaker holds up the Grail Spear and says:

> "This spirited spear is special indeed,
> for dire destiny is deemed from its point;
> the worthy alone can wield it rightly."

4 — Mysteries

Speaker:	"Let the grail mysteries now be spoken."
Speaker:	"Why do you seek the grails?"
Celebrants:	"To become who I am, and I am more than I seem."
Speaker:	"Whom do the grails serve?"
Celebrants:	"They serve myself for Ascent in the cause of Woden."
Speaker:	"Who bears the true Grail Cup?"
Celebrants:	"My fetch to whom I am dedicated."
Speaker:	"What is the true Grail Stone?"

Celebrants:	"My heart that strives to become steadfast and immortal."
Speaker:	"Who wields the true Grail Spear?"
Celebrants:	"My wode-self that I strive to strengthen."

5 — Grail-Work

"From the Grail we drink, that glorious cup:
it is Óðrœrir with awesome mead,
it is Gjallarhorn with greatest wisdom."
"Drink a bounty from this brimming cup."

[Each speaks (silently or out loud) the bounty he desires and then drinks from the Grail.]

"By the Grail we live, that glorious stone:
it is Hrungnir's Heart of holy life,
it is Mímir's Head of hidden matters."
"As a key to your heart, contemplate this stone."

[Each holds the Grail for a few moments.]

"With the Grail we deem, that glorious spear:
it is Gungnir grim for governing wyrd,
it is Gram the sword for gaining renown."
"Work with your wyrd as you wield this spear."

[Each grasps the Grail for a few moments and may speak (silently or out loud) changes to wyrd.]

6 — Leaving

"Through the Grails we've gained; let us go in wisdom
as we strive anew for the stead of their source."

The Good of *Galdralag*: An Inspired Look into Modern Uses for the Meter.

Introduction

Having undertaken an investigation into identifying the instances and uses of the *galdralag* form in the historical poetry (Westcoat, "Goals"), it is time to present practical applications of my discoveries. With *galdralag*, we can enhance our modern religious, magical, and initiatory rites, and we can put the meter to many of the same uses that the ancient poets did. As a secondary objective in this study, integrating the lore into modern poetry is also emphasized. Thus, this exploration of modern uses for *galdralag* will draw heavily on excerpts of poetry I have written. I will first make some brief notes about my modern implementation of the traditional poetic forms. Then I will present the use of *galdralag* for emphasis and indicating magic in drama and storytelling. Next I will cover the use of *galdralag* for short poetic spells and the use of *galdralag* for entering and exiting sacred reality. Following that, I will discuss *galdralag*-like structures in the long lines of *ljóðaháttr* poetry and in non-*ljóðaháttr* poetry. After that, I will return to conventional full line *galdralag* and its applications to initiatory magic, followed by an innovative use of it in the rite of sumbel. Finally, I will blend the *galdralag* meter with all twenty-four rune staves of the Elder Fuþark in a new rune poem called "Rúnagaldraljóð," and then discuss some conclusions.

Notes on My Poetic Forms and Language

It should be noted that, as demonstrated by Geoffrey Russom in *Beowulf and Old Germanic Metre*, different languages will have different realizations of the alliterative lines. Thus, although we use alliterative poetry today, we should not expect nor necessarily desire exact conformance with the syllable structures of our ancestors' poetry — our language today is different from theirs. In that context, I must point out that my *ljóðaháttr* full lines are not exactly the same as those in Old Norse. In particular, I do not necessarily avoid the ending of a long disyllable the way they did (Turville-Petre xv–xvi). More broadly, I do not use syllable length as strictly as they did, as it seems that the modern English ear is not really that attuned to syllable length — for instance, modern English words are not distinguished by the different time length of the vowel pronunciation, whereas in Old English or Old Norse, the time length distinction was often critical. Generally, for my *fornyrðislag*-style poetry, I use half lines containing two stresses each, to make long lines of four stresses in all. Usually, these half lines will have a minimum of four syllables, although some of my earlier poetry has half lines of three syllables. For my *ljóðaháttr*-style poetry, I use long lines just as in *fornyrðislag*, except that the first half line will often be of only three syllables, which was not unusual for the *ljóðaháttr* poetry of the *Poetic Edda*. For the full line, I almost always use three stresses to help differentiate it from a half line or long line. Lastly, it should be noted that all translations in this essay are my own, and all Old Norse quotations of the *Poetic Edda* are from the edition of Neckel and Kuhn.

Magical Emphasis in Storytelling through Galdralag

As I have shown, *galdralag* was certainly used for emphasis (Westcoat, "Goals"), and Ilya Sverdlov has indicated its use in marking significant turning points in a story or drama where magic is involved (60). Now I will give an example to show magic using *galdralag* in a modern ritual drama, just as the poets of *Locasenna* and *Alvíssmál* seem to have done. Here I present two half stanzas of speech from a short, poetic ritual drama I have written about Óðinn's winning of Óðrœrir. In this drama, the characters speak in *ljóðaháttr*. To emphasize two key points in the narrative when Óðinn shape-shifts, I have made his speech into *galdralag* to show that he is using magic (Westcoat, *Viking* 114, 116):

Your duty's done:
I deem that you go.
I shift my shape to sneak,
I shift my shape to snake.

. . . .
My dear Gunnlöð,
I do what I must.
I shift my shape to soar,
I shift my shape to eagle.

In both cases, the *galdralag* lines proceed from Óðinn's desired intent (to sneak or soar) to the physical form that will carry out that intent (snake or eagle).

Many of the stories of the *Prose Edda* have no counterpart in the extant poetry — one of these stories is the forging of the treasures of the gods. I have retold this story as a poem called "The Six Treasures" in *ljóðaháttr* meter and used *galdralag* in two key places, and only these places, to show the exceptional magic involved in the forging of Mjöllnir and the heavy significance of the gods' pronouncement that it is the best of treasures, at the ends of stanzas six and eight respectively (Westcoat, *Viking* 38):

Glowing gold
by gifted Eitri
was forged to dearest Draupnir.
Blazing iron
by brilliant Eitri
was forged to foe of etins,
was forged to mighty Mjöllnir.

. . . .
Óðinn and Thor,
and third was Freyr,
the gods who joined in judgement.
The given verdict,
the greatest treasure:

236

best was bane of etins,
best was mighty Mjöllnir!

As this is a poem intended for recitation and modern audiences are not exceptionally familiar with the *ljóðaháttr* meter, the *galdralag* lines do have notable repetition in them so that they will stand out markedly during recitation.

Short Poetic Spells Using Galdralag

As in the *Hávamál* list of charms, one can use *galdralag* for composing spells in modern English. It should be noted that *galdralag* is not strictly necessary for writing modern spells, of course, as only five of the eighteen *Hávamál* charms have *galdralag* in them, and in *Grógaldr* (found in Bray's edition, but not in Neckel and Kuhn), only one of the nine spells has *galdralag*. Nonetheless, I shall include a demonstration here of such *galdralag*-enhanced spells that also call upon the runes of the Elder Fuþark. (The capitalized words in the second half of each stanza are the means of calling upon the power of particular rune staves for the spell — they are the rune names or ideas translated into modern English, more or less.) From an enumerated series of charms I composed originally in *ljóðaháttr*,[1] I present three of them, modified to use *galdralag*.

> *For Inspiration (Ansuz and Æhwaz)*
> I know a third,
> a thirst it quenches
> when making mead is needful:
> I harked to Óðinn
> and hailed the Yew;
> at first though stuck and still,
> my wode was strongly stirred.
>
> . . . .
> *For Concentration (Isa)*

---

[1] These are the "Staves for the Self" in the Charms and Invocations chapter in this volume.

I know a fourth
to foster will
when focus of mind falters:
to counter chaos
I called on Ice;
from torment hard and troubled
my concentration returned.

. . . .

For Speed in All Things (Raiðo and Ehwaz)
I know a sixteenth
for swiftness sure
if a spell of speed is needed:
I Rode on Horse
and raced with haste;
from start of sluggish snail
my actions all were fast.

The full lines that end the stanzas start from the undesired condition and then transition to the desired state. Here, in each case, the speaker is using magic upon himself. My investigation of *galdralag* noted that scholarly commentary has indicated examples of that, plus examples of using magic for the benefit of others and using magic to harm others (Westcoat, "Goals" 82–83). Using *galdralag* for the benefit of others can easily be done. Indeed, the use of *galdralag* for transitioning from profane reality to sacred reality and its use in initiatory contexts, described in later sections, are examples of just that. Examples of using *galdralag* for cursing or harming others, however, are not included in this work — but that will be no obstacle to the dedicated seeker.

Transitioning to Sacred Reality through Galdralag

As noted in my *galdralag* investigation (Westcoat, "Goals" 74), Elizabeth Jackson's work shows that *galdralag* was used by the poets to suspend the ordinary *ljóðaháttr* meter for the presentation of poetic lists. Alternately stated, they used the meter to set the list

238

apart from the rest of the poem. Any modern poet could easily imitate that usage in a piece of poetry. Here, I will move beyond that idea to something more widely useful. That is, since *galdralag* was used to suspend poetic reality and enter a list, we may use it in ritual to suspend profane reality and enter a sacred reality. I will now present the following examples: setting off a *formáli* in a magical working and the opening and closing of a ritual.

This first usage is one that I have found very psychologically satisfying. In a procedure for creating a magical rune tine, Edred includes a step called the *formáli* in which the tine is given its purpose through an act of significant speech (*Futhark* 115). Such a ritual of rune magic is already set off from the profane world, of course, but I found it helpful to have the *formáli*, as the most significant speech act in the working, further set off from the rest of the rite. To that end, I created a *galdralag* half stanza to mark the start of the *formáli*, and to mark its completion, I created a reversal of it with a reversed *galdralag* that puts the full lines first:

> Wight of my will,
> your work I sing,
> as now I name thy toil,
> as now I deem thy doom.
>
> . . . .
> Now my naming is done,
> now my deeming is done:
> with my might and main
> I made it so.

In the middle between these two *galdralag* half stanzas, in an atmosphere of further enhanced sacredness, I speak the words of purpose that the tine will fulfill.

In this second usage, a piece of *galdralag* is used to effect the change from the profane world to the sacred world for ritual. At the end of the ritual, another *galdralag* is used to return to the profane world. This time, however, the return *galdralag* does not swap the line order, since either approach to the line order may be used as appropriate or desired.

> Wend we now
> our way through rite
> from world of mundane matter
> to world of timeless truth!
> . . . .
> Now we've finished
> and by need return
> from world of holy heights
> to middle world of Man.

In the return call, I have altered the descriptions of the mundane world and sacred world for variety's sake. One can simply reuse the same descriptions from the first *galdralag* in reverse order in the second if that is preferred instead.

Galdralag-like Structures in Long Lines and Elsewhere

As I demonstrated, it may be possible to construe as *galdralag* certain structures in *ljóðaháttr* poems that involve long lines (Westcoat, "Goals" 76–78). Also, I noted that *galdralag*-like forms occur outside of *ljóðaháttr* poetry (Westcoat, "Goals" 71). I will touch on both possibilities here, starting with the former.

As a journey charm for protection that can be used on a friend or loved one, those who prefer Old Norse can simply use Frigg's lines in *Vafþrúðnismál* 4 verbatim.[2] For those who prefer modern English, here is my translation that retains the *ljóðaháttr* meter:

> Heill þú farir,   Hale you go,
> heill þú aptr komir,   hale you come back,
> heill þú á sinnom sér!   hale you on highway be!

---

[2] In the Old Norse the adjective *heill* is in masculine form, because it's spoken to Óðinn. If you speak this to a woman, the form would be *heil* instead. Speaking it to a group of two or more will require further changes to adjective, verb, and pronoun.

240

Here is a slightly different version, still in *ljóðaháttr*, inspired by the *galdralag* of *Hávamál* 156.

> May hale you go,
> and hale you return,
> and hale be after ever!

Both charms make use of the combination of long line (that is, two half lines) plus full line in forming their magic through extended repetition. Although I noted the curious case of consecutive unexpected long lines in *ljóðaháttr* poetry (Westcoat, "Goals" 76–78), an application of that is not included here.

Now for an example of *galdralag*-like structures outside of *ljóðaháttr* poetry. I pointed out stanzas in the lore where magic could be seen as working through the expansion or limitation of the conditions of one line by means of the following line (Westcoat, "Goals" 85–88). This can be worked into non-*ljóðaháttr* poetry in a modern context as well. I have done this in the concluding stanza of my twenty-stanza *fornyrðislag* poem "Yggdrasilsdrápa" (Westcoat, *Viking* 149):

> May Elm and Ash
> give ear to these words:
> Outside and in,
> Yggdrasil is real,
> and may this mead
> give might to both —
> to the Tree without,
> to the Tree within!

The repetitive nature of the last two lines is intended to take the application of the power of the mead (that is, the entire preceding poem which recounts the lore of Yggdrasil) to the external (or universal) World-Tree and expand it to apply to the internal (or particular) World-Tree that is in each woman and man (as emphasized by the Elm and Ash metaphor at the beginning of the stanza). However, it should be noted that since the *fornyrðislag* form only uses one type of line, the long line (which I have broken into half lines here), the surprise of unexpected consecutive full lines that is characteristic of *galdralag* is lacking, even when repetition is used. If an extra, fifth long line is used in a *fornyrðislag* stanza, it could present some surprise, but it would probably not rise to the level of surprise that is found in proper *galdralag*, as the listener is expecting a long line already anyway. A strong marking of boundaries in regular four line stanzas could prepare the way for presenting such a surprise. In my example, an alternate approach is possible, however, in which the last stanza is transformed into a half-stanza of ordinary *fornyrðislag* plus a half stanza of *galdralag*, making the entire poem into a charm. It would be unusual and unnatural, but in recitation I could stress the preposition "to" in each of the last two half lines — this would turn them each into valid full lines of three stress each, and would likely be quite a surprise coming at the end of a poem that has been entirely in *fornyrðislag*! As Sverdlov noted, "a full line is a metrical, not an editorial reality" (53). To that, I would further add that a full line is also a *spoken* reality. All of this demonstrates the possibility for hiding the magic of *galdralag* in forms that would appear to be far removed from it.

Using Galdralag in Initiatory Magic

Both *Hávamál* and *Sigrdrífomál* contain overt initiatory contexts, and both make use of *galdralag* to create more effective initiations (Westcoat, "Goals" 82, 84, 86). To help restore this tradition, I present examples of *galdralag* for modern initiations that could potentially be adapted for use in the rites of the Rune-Gild and in other Germanic Heathen contexts.

As a start, we can fashion memory charms that emphasize the importance of the sacra that we are imparting to the initiates, just as the elder poets did in *Hávamál* and *Sigrdrífomál*. Here is a rather generic example that I have created:

> Remember well
> these mighty sayings,

full of use when used,
full of need when needed.

Also, although no example is given here, we can use *galdralag* to add further emphasis to a particular teaching that we impart to a student, just as the *Hávamál* and *Sigrdrífomál* poets used *galdralag* to add emphasis to key portions in presenting a list of wise counsels (Westcoat "Goals" 84–85). Such *galdralag* could be used in a list that was entirely in *ljóðaháttr*, or perhaps adapted for modern usage in a list that was not in meter except for the *galdralag*. However, my experience in group and interpersonal initiatory contexts is limited — thus the first part of this section is primarily to indicate the potential that exists.

I do have a bit more experience in self-initiatory contexts, however, and can provide two practical examples from that. First, here is the *galdralag* half stanza I used when I coated with linseed oil a stave I had carved with the complete Elder Fuþark:

> I make you glisten
> and gleam with strength
> to work the magic of mystery,
> to work the wonder of initiation.

In the *galdralag* lines, I started from the stave's obvious purpose as something that represents the mysteries and expanded it to include propelling me on my initiatory path. It is, after all, simply putting magic to one of its best and highest uses — that of initiation and self-transformation.

My second example is also one that was intended to propel me on my initiatory path. It is a half stanza that I wrote back in April 2011, before being named a Learner in the Rune-Gild, and before I had any idea that I would undertake a scholarly study of *galdralag*. It was the end to some poetry I wrote about the first four Doors in the curriculum of Edred's *The Nine Doors of Midgard*:

> In composing these poems
> and pouring the mead,

the Learner's synthesis I sought,
the Fellow's threshold I found.

With this, I aimed to channel the power of the whole set of poems (seventy stanzas in all),[3] which were meant to reflect doing the Work of a Learner and accomplishing its aims, into propelling me towards naming as a Fellow in the Rune-Gild. I would venture that they have succeeded in their purpose.

Enhancing Sumbel with Galdralag

It is time to extend the modern use of *galdralag* a bit past what was found in the lore. I have innovated a new way of looking at the *galdralag* full lines — as a way of blending two separate speech acts. The traditional sumbel has three rounds which are well known among modern heathens: a first round to the gods, a second round to heroes and ancestors, and a third round for oaths, boasts and toasts.

I present here a way to craft a sequence of poetic toasts, one for each round, and have the third toast draw and build upon the power of the first two, through reference to them and through the *galdralag* meter. In the cosmological model, the first two toasts can be seen as referencing past action — the layers in the Well of Wyrd. The third toast is then seen as a magic charm that draws upon the power of the first two by referencing their content and by using a *galdralag* structure. This will be much easier to understand by way of an example. The example I present is one that I actually composed and presented in a small sumbel for the magical purpose of enhancing my quest for Óðrœrir. As a note of context, that sumbel immediately followed a blót to Óðinn that specifically celebrated his winning of Óðrœrir.

In the first round toast, I hail a particular god, Óðinn in this case, and refer to his actions in the winning and pouring of the

---

[3] This set of poems was eventually rewritten and expanded to cover the entirety of *The Nine Doors of Midgard*, and it appears as the chapter The Work of Nine Doors in this volume.

poetic mead. In the second round toast, I reference ancestors and heroes — in this case, the poets and scholars who have benefited from Óðinn's Mead. Both of the first two toasts are in *ljóðaháttr*, not *galdralag*. This is done for two reasons. First, as a recounting of the deeds of gods and ancestors, they are not trying to accomplish magic in themselves; hence, I have not used *galdralag* in them. They are, however, trying to set the stage for magic through *galdralag* and that is why I have composed them in the form most similar and resonant to *galdralag* — that of *ljóðaháttr*. Finally, in the third round, I reference elements of both of the first two toasts in weaving together a statement of my magical will. In the third round toast, I have used *galdralag* in each half stanza for working the magic of synthesis and identity. The antecedent in the lore for this is *Sigrdrífomál* 13, where the *galdralag* asserts an identity of a special liquid in declaring:

af þeim legi,	from the liquid
er lekið hafði	that had leaked
ór hausi Heiddraupnis	out of Heiddraupnir's head
oc ór horni Hoddrofnis.	and out of Hoddrofnir's horn.

In the first half stanza of my third round toast, I use *galdralag* to blend together the key aspects of my work — emulating Óðinn and being a skald and scholar — while at the same time drawing upon the first and second toasts respectively. In the second half stanza, I put the focus entirely on Óðinn (the subject of the first toast), and I use the *galdralag* to combine two key aspects of his quest to win the mead — his transformation into a serpent to gain entry to Hnitbjörg, and his transformation into an eagle to escape after obtaining Óðrœrir. In the third half stanza, my focus is entirely on the heroes and ancestors (the subject of my second toast), and I use the *galdralag* to synthesize aspects of the skald and scholar — the wode the skald uses in presenting his poems, and the care and precision with words the scholar uses in presenting his research. In the fourth and final half stanza, I again reference both of the preceding toasts by repeating their two penultimate lines ("For pouring out / precious Óðrœrir") and by using the *galdralag* full lines

245

to combine my own work in poetry and scholarship with my quest to emulate Óðinn and win Óðrœrir for myself. [*The three sumbel toasts are in the Initiatory Sumbel Toasts chapter in this volume, and they are the poem titled "Óðrœrir (January 2012)."*]

Runes and Galdralag

As I had shown, runes were a frequent theme of the extant *galdralag* stanzas in Old Norse poetry (Westcoat, "Goals" 83–84). I also showed that *galdralag* was often used for magical expansion — that the second full line could represent an expansion of the conditions in the first line (Westcoat, "Goals" 86–88). In the poetry previously featured, it may have been noticed that *galdralag* is something for occasional use — a particular spice for stand-alone tastings or to add flavor to a longer poem. Seldom would one feature *galdralag* as the main course by putting it in every stanza of a poem. However, the runes, by way of a rune poem, offer an opportunity for putting *galdralag* in every stanza of a poem and for it to be appropriate. Indeed, it just would not seem right to put *galdralag* in the stanzas for some rune staves and not others. Of course, in maintaining the meter throughout the whole poem, the element of surprise is lost as the audience would quickly come to expect the extra line. However, the pattern that now alternates between long line plus full line and long line plus two full lines may keep the audience attentive and off balance. Yet, as will be seen, opportunities for surprise are still possible. Thus, I have crafted a new rune poem, "Rúnagaldraljóð," designed to take external aspects of the runes and expand them to internal spiritual aspects through the magic of *galdralag* — with an extra *galdralag* line in the Rúna stanza and a key reversal in the final stanza's *galdralag* lines. [*The poem "Rúnagaldraljóð" is in the Rune-Work Poems chapter.*]

246

Conclusions

Through this study, I hope to have demonstrated that the poetic meters of old, most particularly *galdralag* (but also *fornyrðislag* and *ljóðaháttr* as well) can find new life in the modern context of the Germanic Revival. Whether for magic, initiation, ritual, storytelling, drama, or sumbel and beyond, the wise use of *galdralag*, blended with traditional lore, can enhance one's work. I leave the reader with the two final stanzas that set me on road toward Mastery.

> Hale those who read,
> Hale those who understand
> Hale those who deeply drink.
> The lore and myself
> I've linked together
> in writing this stalwart study.

> Hail the Fellow,
> Hail the Master,
> Hail the Holy Gild!
> Through work and wode
> I've waxed in being
> and found the Fellow's grade
> for rising to Master's might.

Works Cited

Bray, Olive, ed. *The Elder or Poetic Edda*. London: Viking Society for Northern Research, 1908. *Viking Society Web Publications*. PDF.

Edred Thorsson. *Futhark: A Handbook of Rune Magic*. York Beach: Weiser, 1984. Print.

———. *The Nine Doors of Midgard*. 5th ed. The Rune-Gild, 2016. Print.

Jackson, Elizabeth. "Eddic Listing Techniques and the Coherence of *Rúnatal*." *Alvíssmál* 5 (1995): 81–106. PDF.

Neckel, Gustav, and Hans Kuhn, eds. *Edda: Die Lieder des Codex Regius nebst verwandten Denkmälern*. 5th ed. Heidelberg: Carl Winter, 1983. Print.

Russom, Geoffrey. *Beowulf and Old Germanic Metre*. Cambridge: Cambridge UP, 1998. Print.

Sverdlov, Ilya V. "Ok dulða ek þann alsvinna jǫtun: Some linguistic and metrical aspects of Óðinn's win over Vafþrúðnir." *Saga-Book* 35 (2011): 39–72. PDF

Turville-Petre, E. O. G. *Scaldic Poetry*. Oxford: Clarendon P, 1976. Print.

Westcoat, Eirik. "The Goals of *Galdralag*: Identifying the Historical Instances and Uses of the Metre." *Saga-Book* 40 (2016): 69–90. Print.

———. *Viking Poetry for Heathen Rites: Asatru Liturgy in Traditional Verse*. Long Branch, PA: Skaldic Eagle Press, 2017. Print.

Runes for the Grails:
Creating Old English Rune Poem Stanzas for Cweorð, Calc, Stān, and Gār.

Introduction

In modern rune craft, we can use the Anglo-Saxon Fuþorc for works of magic and divination, and to aid in this purpose, we have the poetic stanzas of the Old English Rune Poem for twenty-nine of the thirty-three rune staves. Many will be content with that. Others will want to make use of the remaining four staves, Cweorð, Calc, Stān, and Gār. With scarcely more than their names to go on, how is this to be done? Edred Thorsson was clearly not satisfied with this lack, and has done much to develop lore for them that is firmly grounded in the Germanic tradition (*Alu* 137–43). Most interestingly, he even connects the final three, Calc, Stān, and Gār, to the Grail Mythos (*Alu* 205–08). I am quite thankful for that bounty, and without it, this project would be much poorer or perhaps even impossible to finish.

As a poet, however, that lore is not enough for me. I feel that these staves must have poetic stanzas of their own before they can truly be put on equal footing with the other twenty-nine. Furthermore, these stanzas should be in Old English just like the other twenty-nine. This essay is about my quest to create such stanzas and do so in a manner that is as true to the tradition as possible. As I am indeed following Edred in connecting the final three staves to the Grail Mythos, this quest is thus truly a Grail Quest. That is a very tall order for a Fellow of the Rune-Gild, and I shall do my best.[1] In good Gild tradition, such a quest would have to be suitably grounded in the existing traditional sources and proceed according to proper methods so that poetic inspiration could be most fruitfully brought to bear on the problem. It should be noted,

---

[1] That is, I was a Fellow at the time I wrote this essay in the latter half of 2013.

however, that the fruits of this effort are an example, not a dogma. Other valid stanzas for the four runes are possible, and they would be very different if the connection to the Grail Mythos was rejected. Yet another possible approach would be to attempt to write the sort of stanzas that one might expect the original poet to have written. Perhaps I will even write alternate stanzas using such approaches in the future. For now, however, these are my Runes for the Grails.

Inspiration strikes chaotically, and so it should be noted that this essay was not composed in order. Ultimately, however, the chaos must be synthesized into an order. First, I discuss the subject matter that I am using for the innovated stanzas. This will draw heavily on Edred's material, but I will also connect it to Celtic and Grail Mythos material where appropriate as well. Stanzas created for Cweorð, Calc, Stān, and Gār should fit well as an extension of the existing poem, hereafter to be referred to as the OERP. Therefore, I will next look at the characteristics of the OERP to develop guidelines that the innovated stanzas should conform to. These include the technical aspects of line types and rhythms, stanza length, alliteration, and language elements. To assist the analysis of the technical aspects, I prepared a scansion of the OERP according to the system of Bredehoft, based on the text of Halsall, which immediately follows the technical discussion and a brief introduction to the scansion system. Having discussed both subject matter and meter, I then present the innovated stanzas that I have written in Old English, along with a scansion, some notes, and a literal, non-poetic translation. This is then followed by a loose translation of the entire OERP, including my innovated stanzas, into modern English in an alliterative poetic meter. It is also accompanied by some notes on form and vocabulary. Then I present an esoteric analysis of my innovated stanzas. Finally, I will conclude with a brief look at the possibilities that are opened up by this work, for my innovated stanzas are not an end — they are just a beginning.

The Subject Matter of the New Stanzas

Besides meter, alliteration, language, and similar technical aspects, the major issue in innovating the stanzas is determining just what to write about each of the four runes. Also, what audience are they to be aimed at? More fundamentally, what are the new stanzas *for*? As a member of the Rune-Gild, I use runes for their highest and best possible purposes in the modern world: the works of self-transformation, magic, and divination. Thus, I will have an eye toward making the stanzas amenable to that. The author of the OERP was a Christian; I, however, am a Heathen. Therefore, I will not be trying to Christianize the stanzas at all. Instead, I will make more use of overtly heathen material than the OERP author did. Also, my poetic translation of the original twenty-nine stanzas will seek to de-Christianize the material as much as it allows.

Thankfully, much of the heavy work of attaching appropriate lore to the four runes has been done by Edred Thorsson in his recent book *Alu*. His particular approach is one that appeals to me. In developing material for those four staves, he seeks to connect them to Heathen Germanic ideas. From his speculative appendix of triadic rune names, it is also clear that he feels the expanded staves of the Anglo-Saxon Fuþorc should be connected to and rooted in the original system of the Elder Fuþark (*Alu* 203). Thus, I have chosen to follow Edred's approach and rely on his material about the four staves as a starting point for composing my stanzas. As the Grail Mythos material is quite friendly to the work of self-transformation, I am also using his material on the grail runes. Nevertheless, I will go beyond his material in some places, as the astute reader may notice.

In the rest of this section, I will discuss the material I plan to use for the four staves and provide a bit more background on the Grail Mythos since it will be a major theme in the final three stanzas and the Cweorð stanza will serve as a gateway to them. Yet it will still remain for me to apply a poet's touch to the material and to cast it in the language of Old English.

I start here with the material to be used for Cweorð. The meaning of the word is quite uncertain, for it appears nowhere else but in Fuþorc lists that give the names of the runes. Edred gives 'fire-bore' as a possible meaning and relates it to Proto-Germanic *kwernō, meaning 'mill-(stone)' (*Alu* 137). *Kwernō*, of course, led to Old English *cweorn* and Modern English *quern*, both of which mean 'a small hand-mill for grinding grain.' Edred notes, "The stem *kwer-* indicates something which turns or spins or something which receives or takes something else in" (*Alu* 137). Unless I wish to treat *cweorð* as a scribal error for *cweorn*, I have nothing else to go on, so I will follow Edred's interpretation of the name as indicating a fire-drill that creates a need-fire by friction alone without the help of flint and steel.

Both Halsall and Jones (and probably others) concluded that the OERP was the product of a single author who intentionally wrote it as a unified whole with the Ēar stanza deliberately meant as an end to the poem (48–49 and 66, respectively). I agree with this unity and have decided to have my addition to the poem respect this in some fashion. Since I will be having Cweorð follow Ēar, I feel that it needs to have a sort of "but wait, there's more" aspect to it, a way to escape the finality of the grave. Also, with so little to go on for this stave, it seems one can try to get more for it by relating it to the context that it is in. In this case, that would be the runes that precede and follow it in the poem. Putting this all together, I am connecting the stave to a need-fire that would be used for starting a funeral pyre, something that would likely horrify the Christian author of the original poem. However, this has the advantage of deliberately going against the decay and finality of the grave in a way that can be connected to initiatory work. Thus it can serve as gateway to the Grail Mythos in the next three runes. The Heathen Germanic appropriateness of a funeral pyre for a dead man can be seen most spectacularly in the story of Baldur's funeral and Ibn Fadlan's account of a funeral pyre for a Rus chieftain.

The core ideas here are the need-fire (and its self-generated nature), the liberation from matter that cremation implies, and the overcoming of the grave. There are no Germanic mythological fire-drills to connect it to, but that is okay, since referencing mythology is a relatively rare thing in the OERP — the Ing stanza is the only one that obviously does so. Its fire aspects connect it somewhat to Ċēn, which is quite all right, as the sounds are closely related. At this point, there is certainly enough material for a stanza. For my Modern English version of it, however, I will leave the name untranslated. It will still be somewhat vague as to what a Cweorð actually is, but this is merely keeping in line with the state of knowledge about the rune, and it has its precedent in Peorð, about which we are also still mostly in the dark. As will be seen, the skaldic metaphor of human beings as trees proves useful here as well.

Before moving on to the final three runes individually, some remarks on the Grail Mythos as a whole are in order. Eliade notes that the grail literature has the motifs of the initiatory quest (104). More imaginative writers have indeed concurred, such as Ravenscroft, who offers an explication of the Grail as an initiatory quest as it is depicted in an illustration by Basilius Valentinus (71–74). An epic poem such as Wolfram's *Parzival* can take the time to treat such themes in great detail. A particularly Heathen Germanic epic of the Grail Mythos could perhaps be developed as well. Like Eliade and others, I too will connect the Grail to initiatory themes. In the space of the stanzas I am writing, however, I can only make the briefest allusions to a Germanization of the Grail Mythos. Short and potent is the order of the day here. Now I will move on to the cup, the stone, and the spear as they appear in the early extent grail stories and the Celtic antecedents they seem to have, along with a discussion of how I am connecting them to the Germanic tradition.

The cup comes first. *Calc*, as a Latin loanword taken into Old English, means 'goblet, cup, or chalice.' Edred is surely right in that this would have meant the cup of the Eucharist for a medieval Christian audience (*Alu* 138). Here I will follow Edred in considering the drinking horn as the heathen version of the chalice. The cultural and mythic associations that Edred then connects it to follow quite naturally: the ritual of sumbel and Óðrœrir, the stirrer of poetry, which is the name of both the cauldron and the mead it contains. The mead of poetry is sometimes connected to the soma of the

Vedas, a drink that brings immortality, as Puhvel has noted, because of certain structural similarities in the stories of how they were obtained (65).

Now for some remarks on the Grail Mythos and Celtic antecedents that I am connecting it with. In the earliest extant grail story, Chrétien de Troyes depicts the grail as a serving dish that brings a consecrated Mass wafer to the Fisher King's father (417). The wafer sustains him and keeps him alive, but it does not heal his sickness. Brown connects this serving dish to the Celtic legend of the Dagda's mighty and bottomless cauldron (35). The grail as dish, of course, would seem to be that which was eventually Christianized into the cup of Jesus from the Last Supper, which is said to give eternal life to those who drink from it.

The core idea here is a container that produces a wonderful bounty. It contains something that is good to consume and transforms those who consume it. It is no stretch at all to see initiatory motifs in such a drink, and these ideas connect well to the horn as exemplified in the Germanic concepts of sumbel and Óðrœrir. Finally, another interesting piece of information that we can make use of is provided by Hollowell. She cites Werlich and says, "Evidence is provided to show that the *woðbora*, raised to religious ecstasy and poetic inspiration through ceremonial drinking of holy mead, at one time performed in the service of a pagan Germanic religious cult" (317). Hollowell has much more to say about the *woðbora*, an obscure figure in the Old English corpus, but here I need only note that the fundamental etymology of the word implies an original reference to a bearer of *wōþ* (327). That *wōþ* is cognate to the *óð*- root in Óðrœrir, so the connections (whether potential or actual, poetical or etymological) hardly need to be commented on.

The stone comes next. *Stān* is a very widely attested word and simply means 'stone.' In the Germanic tradition, Edred notes that stone was used for altars, memorials, and grave-markers, and he considers permanence and eternity as two of its important characteristics (*Alu* 140).

254

Chrétien's story does not have a stone, but Wolfram's features a stone as the Grail itself (198). Brown connects Wolfram's stone to the Lia Fail (35). That Celtic stone would identify the rightful king of Ireland by roaring under him. Similarly, Wolfram's stone identifies the individuals who are to serve the grail by displaying their names and lineages in some kind of writing on itself (198). For Murphy, the Grail is a consecrated altar stone, especially of the kind used in portable altars which were needed for celebrating Mass on the road, and this stone is connected to the Christian Holy Sepulcher, the most significant stone in that mythology (36–38). Murphy observes that Wolfram describes the stone in terms of the phoenix mythology and says, "It is the stone that makes death . . . into a molting of feathers. With the new feathers, the soul flies again" (173–74). So the stone is more than just a sign of permanence on its own — it is a means of imparting a permanence and eternity to the soul as well.

Here is where I make a significant departure from the existing Grail Mythos. The various stories all depict only a single grail, whether it is a dish, stone, or cup. The spear seems to be along for the ride and is not reckoned a grail as far as I know. However, I will reckon each of the three — cup, stone, and spear — as a grail. This further serves my purpose of making a particularly Heathen Germanic interpretation of the Grail Mythos, as many significant things occur in threes in the Germanic tradition.

The core ideas here involve the permanence of stone, its ability to impart that eternity to a soul, its ability to make things hallowed or sacred, and its ability to communicate, whether through making a sound or displaying writing of some sort on its surface. In the Germanic mythology, we do not have an obvious candidate for the grail stone. We have a not-so-obvious candidate, however: Hrungnir's heart. Snorri says, "Hrungnir had a heart that is renowned, made of solid stone and spiky with three points just like the symbol for carving called Hrungnir's heart has ever since been made" (78). Simek connects this to the valknut which can be seen on various old picture stones (163). It is not at all obvious, however, what those picture stones have to do with Hrungnir, although they are a case of the valknut being present in Odinic contexts. Am I suggesting that we see Hrungnir's heart as a mythological object? Yes, although more significantly, I am suggesting that Snorri's statement implies Hrungnir's heart as a kenning for the valknut, in which case the valknut should be seen as stone of some sort.[2] Regardless of the valknut connection, we can see Hrungnir's heart as a kenning for a stone *par excellence*, and Wolfram's grail is certainly one of those. We may also note that the tale of Thor's duel with Hrungnir contains apparent initiatory elements. Their existence in the tale is most glaring in the bizarre presence of Mökkurkálfi, whose mare's heart was apparently important enough to mention as well. Ultimately, Hrungnir's heart is won by Thor for the gods through the duel, though Snorri does not tell us what was done with it. Finally, in a separate section, Snorri notes that a heart may be called a stone, among other things (154).

Although I will not use it, we may note another mythological object that has something in common with Wolfram's grail: Mímir's head. It communicates hidden things, but presumably through sound and not through writing. It is not a stone, of course, but it is stone-like in that it has been made immortal by Óðinn so that it does not rot. Outside of mythological objects, we have the runestones left behind by the ancient runemasters, and these fit quite well. They are a way of conferring a sort of immortality through heathen writings by keeping the memory of a deceased person alive, and they could easily be seen as hallowing the location they are in.

The spear comes last. *Gár* is also well attested and means 'spear, javelin, dart.' Spears are quite significant in Germanic culture. Edred notes that the spear is a way to extend power beyond the personal sphere, a sign of sovereignty, and the tool of choice for human sacrifice, whether by actually doing the killing or by magically

---

[2] In my article for the journal *Odroerir*, "The Valknut: Heart of the Slain?", I explored the connection of Hrungnir's heart to the valknut further. In it, I concluded that the 'stone' which the valknut represents is the heart of a brave warrior. Writing that article also had a profound initiatory effect on me — it would be included in this volume, except that I have chosen not to reprint my already-published scholarly works here.

dedicating the victims; it would also be shaken to vote in the assembly (*Alu* 140–42). These uses all indicate a power to alter *wyrd* in one form or another.

Chrétien's grail is preceded by a lance that bleeds a single drop of blood, which seems to be portrayed as having a standing equal to the grail itself (379). Wolfram's grail is also associated with a bleeding lance, but his produces more blood, and the attendees in the hall weep at its sight (98). The Christian impulse would be, of course, to assimilate this lance to the spear of the Crucifixion. Brown, however, points out that the lance in the early Grail Mythos is very much non-Christian (2). He connects it to predecessors in Celtic myth, most notably the spear of Lugh (57). Brown also notes the tale of Balin and the Dolorous Stroke from Malory's *Morte Darthur*, in which Balin grabs the sacred lance and wounds King Pellean with it, magically resulting in widespread destruction in the realm surrounding the location of the incident (42–48). He considers the tale to have many pagan Celtic attributes (49). The Luin is another legendary Celtic spear that he connects it to, one that is venomous, fiery, associated with blood, and wreaks great destruction (21–24). Ravenscroft relates a piece of fanciful Christian mythology, where is said that the Roman centurion who held the spear at the Crucifixion held the destiny of the whole world in his hands, supposedly because had he chosen to break the legs of Jesus (as was customary of crucifixion victims) instead of stabbing him, he would have totally invalidated Jesus as the Christ, apparently on the grounds that it was absolutely essential that not a single bone of him would be broken (ix–xii).

The core ideas involve a capacity for great destruction, immense power, sovereignty, significant choice, and changing the destiny of the self and/or the world. It is connected to blood, bloodshed, and dedicating humans to death. In *Ynglinga saga*, the spear is used to dedicate someone on their deathbed to join Óðinn in the afterlife (13). The strong association with the grail in the early stories justifies putting the spear on an equal footing with the grail — thus my designation of the spear as the third grail in my Germanization

257

of the Grail Mythos. The most significant and well-known spear in the Norse mythology is the one belonging to Óðinn. It is called Gungnir and was forged by a group of dwarves, the sons of Ívaldi. Snorri says that it "never stopped in its thrust" (97). Óðinn also cast a spear over the Vanir armies to start the first war, and was pierced by a spear during his initiation on Yggdrasil to gain the runes.

From all of this, I can set out my approach to extending the OERP. I treat the first twenty-eight runes as representing the various joys and travails of earthly existence. Rune twenty-nine is the grave, the ultimate end of the uninitiated. Rune thirty is the fire-drill, which lights the need-fire to liberate the soul from the constraints of matter so that it may soar into realms beyond. Runes thirty-one through thirty-three are the holy grails, aspects of a spiritual initiatory path which goes beyond the mundane world to the realm of myth. This will be borne out by the strong mythic references in their stanzas, which is unusual compared to the rest of the poem. Also, where most of the staves of the OERP seem to be described in general terms, my grail stanzas will make it clear that a very specific cup, stone, and spear are being referenced. Before I can present my innovated stanzas, a discussion of the technical aspects that they need to conform to must come first.

The Technical Characteristics of the OERP

The raw material of subject matter for the staves must now be put into the proper form. That form, of course, is the one used by the OERP poet. To get a good idea of what the existing stanzas are like, one must make a technical analysis of the OERP. In analyzing the OERP, the text that I will use is the edition of Halsall. The technical aspects I will analyze are the line types and rhythms, stanza length, alliteration, and language elements.

First is the matter of line types and their rhythms. The lines of the OERP are mostly the standard Germanic long line. The stanzas of Hæġl and Nȳd, however, are an exception to this. They consist of so-called hypermetric lines which are longer than typical lines. The system of Sievers, with a few modifications, has been used for scanning Old English verse for over a century. It has had its share of critics, and recently, a new formalism for Old English meter has been developed by Bredehoft. In his system, like previous systems, the standard long line is made of two half lines that are in turn composed of two feet (22). The feet however, are patterned on the stress contours of typical Old English words, and certain rules are used for combining the feet into half lines (verses) and then combining the half lines into long lines. In Bredehoft's system, a hypermetric line is seen to consist of three feet in each of its half lines and has its own rules for how feet and verses may be combined to form lines (52). It is not clear why the OERP poet felt the need to use hypermetric lines. As they occur in only two out of twenty-nine stanzas (four lines out of ninety-four), I do not feel there is any need to use them in my innovated stanzas. Thus my innovated stanzas will use the standard long line. To gain an understanding of the meter of the OERP, I have produced a scansion of it according to Bredehoft's system. The next two sections present a more detailed introduction to the scansion system and then the scansion itself. I used this scansion as a guide for the rest of this technical analysis and for producing verses that conform to the metrical norms of the OERP.

Some comments on the rhythms in the scansion are in order here. A variety of half line types are seen throughout the poem, and my innovated stanzas use only line types that appear in the OERP. However, a careful reader will be able to see that I have implemented some of those types in unusual ways. Most notable is perhaps the use of four monosyllable words at the start of my Calc stanza. It is seen that anacrusis occurs only once in the poem, in line 11b. Thus, my own stanzas should use it sparingly, if at all. Also, it should be noted that the poet is not shy about using finite verbs to alliterate in the b-verse. He does this 8 times out of 90, which to me seems very much more frequent than what can be found in *Beowulf*. (I did not include the hypermetric lines in that count. There are also a few non-alliterating finite verbs that start some of the b-verses.) Thus I need not be shy about doing it in my own stanzas. Nonetheless, I only alliterate one of my 15 b-verses with a finite verb.

Now I turn to the matter of stanza length. The other rune poems feature consistent lengths: the Old Norwegian Rune Poem (ONRP) has two lines of a *dróttkvætt* variant for each rune, while the Old Icelandic Rune Poem (OIRP) has a half stanza of *ljóðaháttr* for each rune. The OERP differs from this, varying the number of lines devoted to each rune. It is as low as two (hypermetric) lines for Hægl and Nȳd and as high as five in the unique case of Ēar. Between those extremes, 19 runes have three lines, and 7 runes have four lines. Clearly, the poet was not obsessed with consistency in this regard. My first instinctive explanation for this is that the poet simply said what he felt he needed to say with however many lines he happened to use. Halsall, however, considers that the poet may have deliberately adjusted the stanzas lengths to mark the ends and starts of the *ættir*, to add variety, and in the case of Ēar, to make a solid conclusion to the poem (50–52). I have already ruled out the use of hypermetric lines in my innovations, so I will not be writing any two-line stanzas. As the five lines of Ēar are rather exceptional, I will not use any five-line stanzas. Thus I will preserve the singularly heavy aspect given to the grave in the poem. That leaves me with stanzas of either three or four lines. I will make the stanzas for Calc, Stān, and Gār have four lines each, to emphasize their equality and significance as the three grails. Cweorð will only have three lines, and such brevity suits its subject matter as well as providing a contrast to the longer stanzas before and after it.

Now I consider alliteration. In the OERP, it is seen that 100 percent of time, the stave name participates in the alliteration of the first line of its stanza. Also, triple alliteration in those first lines is the rule, occurring in 27 out of 29 stanzas. Only Wynn and Peorð have mere double alliteration. (This is in marked contrast to both the OIRP and the ONRP, where the stave name participates in the first line alliteration only 25 and 31 percent of the time, respectively.) Thus, the stave names in my innovated stanzas must participate in the alliteration of their respective first lines. Triple alliteration is preferred, and that is what I use for each of them. All the stanzas in all three rune poems start with the rune name, so my innovative stanzas must do so as well. All are in the nominative case, with the lone exception of the OERP's stanza for Wynn, which uses the stave name in the genitive case as *wynne*. Thus I do have a precedent for using a non-nominative form to open a stanza, but as it is so unusual, I do not do so.

Continuing further on the matter of alliteration, it is necessary to address the distinctiveness of the sounds involved. In writing the Ċēn stanza, the OERP poet clearly did not consider the sounds of |ċ|, |c|, and |cw| to be distinct for alliterative purposes as he makes the triple alliteration in that first line using one of each! However, the rise of Calc as a stave for specifically the |c| sound indicates that a distinction between |ċ| and |c| was developing. We see something similar at work in the Ġyfu and Ġēr stanzas as they both have |ġ| alliterating with |g|. Parallel to Calc, we have the rise of Gār as a stave specifically for the |g| sound. The creation of Cweorð as a stave specifically for |cw| suggests a similar process at work for that sound. Therefore, I will incorporate this distinctiveness of sound into my innovated stanzas by having Cweorð, Calc, and Gār alliterate only with |cw|, |c|, and |g| respectively in their respective first lines. (Note that Halsall's text does not indicate the differences among |ċ|, |c|, |ġ|, and |g|, except where they start the rune names.)

Now I address the alliteration for Stān. It is a well-established ancient Germanic principle that the sounds |st|, |sc|, and |sp| only alliterate with themselves and never with each other or |s|, whereas |s| will alliterate with other initial |s| clusters such as |sw|. We certainly see this in the Norse tradition, and it is apparent in the English as well. In the OERP, this principle is never violated, and |s| is only alliterated with itself and |sw|. The sole instance of alliteration that involves |st|, |sc|, or |sp| is found in the Æsc stanza (line 82) and is a triple alliteration on |st|, suggesting that the author of the OERP stuck with that part of the tradition as well. Thus, in composing a stanza for Stān, I will follow suit, and only alliterate it with other |st| words.

Some notes on rare secondary alliteration are in order. It is present in interesting ways in the OERP. By secondary alliteration, I mean that there is an additional set of alliterating stresses (on a different sound) linking the two half lines. This feature only occurs in six lines of the poem. The instances in lines 12, 40, and 92 seem rather ordinary, and we may wonder if they were accidental or deliberate in order to draw attention to the stanzas for Ōs, Peorð, and Ēar, respectively. However, lines 36 and 37 cannot be an accident as they are quite extraordinary. Each features triple alliteration on the primary sound, yet also has a pair of secondary alliterating sounds. It would seem that such exceptional poetics might have been devised to draw attention to the importance of the yew in the poem. Each of my grail rune stanzas will contain some exceptional poetics in them to accentuate their importance. Line 27 also has secondary alliteration similar to line 36, but the poet had more room for it in a hypermetric line, where it perhaps emphasizes Nȳd.

Lastly, I present some language notes. The most common verb in the first line of each stanza is *byþ*, which means 'is,' although Halsall notes a better rendering of the meaning, though more clunky, would be 'is, was, and ever shall be' (101). My own translation of the original stanzas is intended to be poetic, so I will stick with 'is.' I considered using 'be' instead, but that would sound very odd to the modern ear. Exceptions to the use of *byþ* are the stanzas for Wynn and Eolhx, which use the verbs *brūceþ* and *hæfþ*, respectively. The Ing stanza uses *wæs*, but that is simply the past tense of *byþ*. Of the stanzas using *byþ*, it is always the second word, except in the Ġyfu and Siġel stanzas. Thus although we should expect my innovated stanzas to use *byþ* as the second word, there is some precedent for other possibilities. I am, however, going to stick with *byþ* as the second word of each stanza. When the poet employs a kenning-like genitive construction, he usually puts the genitive noun first. Only in line 36b does he put the genitive noun, *fȳres*, second. However, I will use constructions like that a bit more frequently.

I have written much here about the first line of each stanza. As for the lines after the first, there seems to be no common thread. The poet simply goes on with whatever he needs to say, however he might like to say it, as the subsequent lines do not have to match the alliteration of the first line. Before I present the scansion I have produced and used, a brief introduction to the scansion system will be helpful for many.

A Brief Introduction to the Scansion System I Use Here

The scanning of ancient verse (that is, determining the stress and alliteration patterns) is ultimately an essential exercise for the advanced poetic magicians working in the Germanic tradition, as it will help them get into the mindset of the old poets and how they approached their verse. It will also give them new insights for composing modern verse. As most of my readers are probably not familiar with such scansions, I will briefly introduce the scansion system I use here, which is that of Bredehoft. It is relatively recent, so it has not caught on as much as it deserves to, especially as it is an improvement over the arbitrariness and abstractness of the system developed by Sievers over a hundred years ago. (I do not have space here to explain the Sievers system.) In my scansion of the OERP below, the reader will see things like "Sx/Ss::x/Ssx" and "SA::xC" with each line. This is the scansion of the line in terms of syllables, feet, and verses, and this I will explain, but I do not have the space to explain much more than that.

First, classical Old English poetry deals with "syllable equivalents." These are just syllables as we understand them today, with one special exception (to be mentioned shortly). Stressed syllables typically needed to be "long" syllables into order to count as syllables for metrical purposes. Usually, the root syllable of a word bears the stress. (Prefixes are generally unstressed, but *un-* is a notable exception.) If a word is a compound, the root syllable of the second element will still have some stress, but not as much as the first element. Other syllables will be unstressed. In a one-syllable word, the syllable is long if it ends in a consonant or a long vowel (which is indicated by a macron over it). Thus, *feoh* and *rād* count as long syllables, while *ðe* is short. In a two-syllable word, the last consonant after the vowel is considered to belong to the next syllable. Thus for *fīra*, it is split into syllables for scansion purposes as *fī-ra*, and the first syllable counts as long because it has a long vowel, while the second syllable is short. The word *manna* splits as *man-na*, and the word *byrneþ* splits as *byr-neþ*, and thus each has a long first syllable. However, *wraþu* is split as *wra-þu*, thus giving it two short syllables. This is where the special exception, called "resolution," comes in. Since the first syllable of *wraþu* is both short and stressed, it can be "lumped together" with the immediately following syllable, and the two are thus treated instead as a single long syllable for the purposes of scansion. Typically, resolution is taken to occur whenever possible. However, there are some cases in which it is "suspended" (also called "blocked") — these are when resolution would make an unmetrical verse (such as causing the syllable count to go below the mandatory minimum of four), or when it would change the verse type (discussed a bit below.)

Now some scansion symbols may be introduced. A fully-stressed syllable (or resolved equivalent) is represented by "S", such as *feoh* in line 1a and *wraþu* in line 11b. An unstressed syllable is represented by "x" regardless of length, such as *byþ* in line 1a and *ðe* in line 9b. A partially-stressed syllable (or resolved equivalent) is represented by "s" — these are typically second elements in a compound, but are also root syllables of finite verbs in some cases, such as the second syllable of *anmōd* in line 4a and *sceal* in line 2a, respectively. The "/" simply indicates the foot boundary. I use "::" to represent the caesura between the two verses of a line.

I move on to feet. Bredehoft uses the word-foot approach first developed by Russom for Old English verse, in which the allowable metrical feet are simply based on the stress patterns of words in the language. Thus, a word like *frōfur* in line 1a is an "Sx" foot consisting of a stressed syllable followed by an unstressed syllable, and this is the most common foot. Each verse must have two feet (except for the hypermetric verses which have three, which are in lines 25–28 in the poem). Individual words can be combined into compound feet where appropriate — thus *feoh byþ* in line 1a is scanned as an "Sx" foot just like *frōfur* after it. And thus line 1a has its two feet and "Sx/Sx" is its scansion. (In such compound feet, something that would normally be an "S" may be scanned with "s" instead, like in a compound word.) In line 11a, *wīsdōmes* is "Ssx" in three syllables. (It is *wīs* with a partially-stressed derivational suffix, *-dōm*, so it is like a compound word here.) It is followed by *wraþu*, which is resolved and thus an "S," making the verse "Ssx/S." For each of the lines, the verse type is listed to the right. These are "SA" for line 1a and "CsS" for line 11a. These verse types are classifications given by Bredehoft for grouping together lines of similar scansion. They are relevant for suspended resolution. One may take line 6a as an example. I have scanned it here as "Sx/Ssx" and type "SC." In the compound word *mōr-stapa*, one might expect *stapa* to be resolved. But that would make the scansion "Sx/Ss" and change the verse type to "SA," and thus resolution is suspended. (How to assign a particular scansion to a verse type will not be treated here — the interested reader will have to consult Bredehoft's book.) Lastly, the reader will also notice either "(x)" or "(xx)" or "(xxx)" in certain places. These are extra-metrical syllables (always unstressed) which don't count towards the foot or verse type. They may occur more or less freely before the second foot of any verse and, less commonly, before the first foot (where they are considered to be anacrusis). Note that unstressed prefixes are often treated as extrametrical (*ge-* in line 13b) or even as part of a preceding foot (*ge-* in line 44b).

Unfortunately, these comments will not suffice to explain all possible details of my treatment of words and syllables in the scansion to the lay reader, who will doubtless still find something confusing. But they will at least allow the reader to get a beginning idea of the nature of the rhythm of the poetry and how it is put together, as well as the intricacies of scanning it.

The Text and Scansion of the OERP

Here I present the text of Halsall (86–92), along with a scansion according to the system of Bredehoft. I have consulted the scansion of Jones (124–29), who used the system of Sievers. I have made only five changes to the text of Halsall. For the lacuna in line 39a, I have inserted Dobbie's emendation "*and wīsum*" as reported by Halsall to render it complete and metrically valid (129). My second change is that I do not put the rune names in parentheses, and I capitalize them all. My third change is emending *niþa* to *niþða* in line 27b on metrical grounds to make the word a natural Sx foot. The alternatives are either suspending resolution or scanning the last two feet as S/Sx. As a comparative note, we find this form with a long consonant twice in *Beowulf*, once naturally as *niþða* (line 1005), a second time emended to *niðða* from the short form *niða* (line 2215). Emendation and consonant length aside, in each of those cases the word is certainly being treated as Sx, whether naturally or by suspended resolution. However, like those editors, I prefer emending to the long consonant. My fourth change is emending *ēst* to *eft* in line 68b; Halsall notes that this has been done by others (147). This does not affect the scansion of that line, however. I am basing my poetic translation on this text, and the Peorð and Ing emendations are important to it. Lastly, I have not reproduced the italicized letters from her text, which indicated where she emended the text of Hickes. Instead, I have reserved italics for the things that I have changed from her text, and I have italicized the whole word where a change was made instead of a just a letter in order to avoid confusing my readers.

A note on *ungemetum* is in order here. The proper scansion of this word in the OERP does not seem obvious. I am treating it as Sxxx instead of Sxs, to avoid a verse pattern of Sxs/Sx in line 8b, as Bredehoft does not allow Sxs in the first foot of a normal verse (27). He does not exclude Sxx from the first foot of a normal verse there, and so I am not excluding Sxxx either. For consistency, I then consider *ungemetum* to also be Sxxx when it recurs in line 29b. Resolution is probably suspended on *slidor* there and thus it is an SA verse also. (If it is treated as a single syllable due to resolution or the disregard of an epenthetic vowel, it would change the verse type to a CxS verse of Sxxx/S, which is still okay, although unusual.) However line 8b is reckoned, I consider it valid, and line 109a in my extension is metrically identical to it. I also note that constructions with extra-metrical syllables, such as Sxx/(x)S or Sx/(xx)Sx do seem to be allowed in Old English verse (though the former would be quite rare), and my treatment of *ungemetum* produces verses with stress patterns identical to those. Primary alliteration is indicated with underline (S and s) and secondary alliteration is indicated with double underline (S and s). (As the double underlines are few, I note that they only occur in lines 12, 27, 36, 37, 40, and 92.)

1	Feoh byþ frōfur fīra gehwylcum;	Sx/Sx::Sx/(x)Sx	SA::SA
	sceal ðēah manna gehwylc miclun hyt dǣlan,	sx/Sxxs::Sx/(x)Sx	sB::SA
	gif hē wile for Drihtne dōmes hlēotan.	xxsx/Sx::Sx/Sx	sA::SA
	Ūr byþ anmōd and oferhyrned,	Sx/Ss::x/Ssx	SA::xC
5	felafrēcne dēor — feohteþ mid hornum —	Ssx/S::Sx/(x)Sx	CsS::SA
	mǣre mōrstapa; þæt is mōdig wuht!	Sx/Ssxx::xx/Sxs	SC::xB
	Ðorn byþ ðearle scearp, ðegna gehwylcum	Sx/Sxs::Sx/(x)Sx	SB::SA
	anfengys yfyl, ungemetun rēþe	Ssx/S::Sxxx/Sx	CsS::SA
	manna gehwylcun ðe him mid resteð.	Sx/(x)Sx::xx/Ssx	SA::xC
10	Ōs byþ ordfruma ǣlcre sprǣce,	Sx/Ssx::Sx/Sx	SC::SA
	wīsdōmes wraþu and witena frōfur	Ssx/S::(x)Sx/Sx	CsS::SA
	and eorla gehwām ēadnys and tōhiht.	x/Sxxs::Sx/(x)Ss	xB::SA
	Rād byþ on recyde rinca gehwylcum	Sx/(x)Sx::Sx/(x)Sx	SA::SA
	sēfte, and swīþhwæt ðām ðe sitteþ onufan	Sx/(x)Ss::xx/Sxxs	SA::xB
15	mēare mægenheardum ofer mīlpaþas.	Sx/Ssx::xx/Ssx	SC::xC
	Ċēn byþ cwicera gehwām cūþ on fȳre,	Sx/Sxxs::Sx/Sx	SB::SA
	blāc and beorhtlīc; byrneþ oftust	Sx/Ss::Sx/Sx	SA::SA
	ðǣr hī æþelingas inne restaþ.	xx/Ssx::Sx/Sx	xC::SA
	Ġyfu gumena byþ gleng and herenys	S/Sxs::Sx/Sx	SB::SA
20	wraþu and wyrþscype; and wrǣcna gehwām	Sx/Ssx::x/Sxxs	SC::xB
	ār and ætwist, ðe byþ ōþra lēas.	Sx/Ss::xx/Sxs	SA::xB

Wynne brūceþ   ðe can wēana lȳt,   Sx/Sx::xx/Sxs   SA::xB
sāres and sorge,   and him sylfa hæfþ   Sx/(x)Sx::xx/Sxs   SA::xB
blǽd and blysse   and ēac byrga geniht.   Sx/Sx::xx/Sxxs   SA::xB

25 Hægl byþ hwītust corna;   hwyrft hit of heofones lyfte,
                        Sx/Sx/Sx::sx/(x)Sx/Sx   SSS::sSS
wealcaþ hit windes scūra;   weorþeþ hit tō wætere syððan.
                        sx/(x)Sx/Sx::sx/(xx)Sx/Sx   sSS::sSS

Nȳd byþ nearu on brēostan;   weorþeþ hī ðēah oft *niþða* bearnum
                        Sx/Sx/Sx::sx/(xxx)Sx/Sx   SSS::sSS
tō helpe and tō hǽle gehwæþre,   gif hī his hlystaþ ǽror.
                        (x)Sx/(xx)Sx/(x)Sx::xxx/Sx/Sx   SSS::xSS

Īs byþ oferceald,   ungemetum slidor;   Sx/Ss::Sxxx/Sx   SA::SA
30 glisnaþ glæshlūttur   gimmum gelīcust;   sx/Ssx::Sx/(x)Sx   sC::SA
flōr forste geworuht,   fæger ansȳne.   S/Sxxs::S/Ssx   SB::SC

Ġēr byþ gumena hiht,   ðon God lǽteþ,   Sx/Sxs::x/Ssx   SB::xC
hālig heofones cyning,   hrūsan syllan   Sx/Sxs::Sx/Sx   SB::SA
beorhte blēda   beornum and ðearfum.   Sx/Sx::Sx/(x)Sx   SA::SA

35 Ēoh byþ ūtan   unsmēþe trēow,   Sx/Sx::Ssx/S   SA::CsS
heard hrūsan fæst,   hyrde fȳres,   S/Sxs::Sx/Sx   SB::SA
wyrtrumun underwreþyd,   wynan on ēþle.   Ss/Sxs::Sx/Sx   SB::SA

Peorð byþ symble   plega and hlehter   Sx/Sx::Sx/Sx   SA::SA
wlancum *and wīsum*,   ðār wigan sittaþ   Sx/(x)Sx::x/Ssx   SA::xC
40 on bēorsele   blīþe ætsomne.   x/Ssx::Sx/(x)Sx   xC::SA

Eolhxsecg eard hæfþ   oftust on fenne,   Ss/Ss::Sx/(x)Sx   SA::SA
wexeð on wature;   wundaþ grimme,   sx/Sx::Sx/Sx   sA::SA
blōde brēneð   beorna gehwylcne   Sx/Sx::Sx/(x)Sx   SA::SA
ðe him ǽnigne   onfeng gedēð.   xx/Sxx::Ssx/S   xC::CsS

45 Sigel sēmannum   symble biþ on hihte,   S/Ssx::Sx/(xx)Sx   SC::SA
ðonn hī hine feriaþ   ofer fisces beþ,   xx/(xx)Sx::xx/Sxs   xA::xB
oþ hī brimhengest   bringeþ tō lande.   xx/Ssx::Sx/(x)Sx   xC::SA

Tīr biþ tācna sum;   healdeð trȳwa wel   Sx/Sxs::sx/Sxs   SB::sB
wiþ æþelingas;   ā biþ on færylde   x/Ssx::Sx/(x)Sx   xC::SA
50 ofer nihta genipu;   nǽfre swīceþ.   xx/Sxxs::Sx/Sx   xB::SA

Beorc byþ blēda lēas;   bereþ efne swā ðēah   Sx/Sxs::Ssx/(x)S   SB::CsS
tānas būtan tūdder;   biþ on telgum wlitig,   Sx/(xx)Sx::xx/Sxs   SA::xB
hēah on helme,   hrysted fægere;   Sx/Sx::Sx/Sx   SA::SA
geloden lēafum,   lyfte getenge.   x/Ssx::Sx/(x)Sx   xC::SA

Eh byþ for eorlum	æþelinga wyn,	S̲x/(x)S̲x::S̲sx/S	SA::CsS
hors hōfum wlanc,	ðǣr him hæleþas ymb,	S̲/S̲xs::xx/S̲xs	SB::xB
welege on wicgum,	wrixlaþ sprǣce;	S̲x/(x)S̲x::S̲x/Sx	SA::SA
and biþ unstyllum	ǣfre frōfur.	xx/S̲sx::S̲x/Sx	xC::SA

Man byþ on mygþe	his māgan lēof;	S̲x/(x)S̲x::x/S̲xs	SA::xB
60 sceal þēah ānra gehwylc	ōðrum swīcan,	sx/S̲xxs::S̲x/Sx	sB::SA
for ðām Dryhten wyle	dōme sīne	xx/S̲xs::S̲x/Sx	xB::SA
þæt earme flǣsc	eorþan betǣcan.	x/S̲xs::S̲x/(x)Sx	xB::SA

Lagu byþ lēodum	langsum geþūht,	S̲x/S̲x::S̲xx/S	SA::CxS
gif hī sculun nēþun	on nacan tealtum,	xxs/S̲x::x/S̲sx	sA::xC
65 and hī sǣyþa	swyþe brēgaþ,	xx/S̲sx::S̲x/Sx	xC::SA
and se brimhengest	brīdles ne gȳmeð.	xx/S̲sx::S̲x/(x)Sx	xC::SA

Ing wæs ǣrest	mid Ēast-Denum	S̲x/S̲x::x/S̲sx	SA::xC
gesewen secgun,	oþ hē siððan *eft*	x/S̲sx::xx/S̲xs	xC::xB
ofer wǣg gewāt;	wǣn after ran;	xx/S̲xs::S̲/Sxs	xB::SB
70 ðus heardingas	ðone hæle nemdun.	x/S̲sx::xx/S̲sx	xC::xC

Ēþel byþ oferlēof	ǣghwylcum men,	S̲x/S̲s::S̲sx/S	SA::CsS
gif he mōt ðǣr rihtes	and gerysena on	xxsx/S̲x::xx/S̲xs	sA::xB
brūcan on bolde	blēadum oftast.	S̲x/(x)S̲x::S̲x/Sx	SA::SA

Dæg byþ Drihtnes sond,	dēore mannum,	S̲x/S̲xs::S̲x/Sx	SB::SA
75 mǣre Metodes lēoht,	myrgþ and tōhiht	S̲x/S̲xs::S̲x/Ss	SB::SA
ēadgum and earmum,	eallum brīce.	S̲x/(x)S̲x::S̲x/Sx	SA::SA

Āc byþ on eorþan	elda bearnum	S̲x/(x)S̲x::S̲x/Sx	SA::SA
flǣsces fōdor;	fereþ gelōme	S̲x/S̲x::S̲x/Sx	SA::SA
ofer ganotes bæþ;	— garsecg fandaþ	xx/S̲xs::S̲s/Sx	xB::SA
80 hwæþer āc hæbbe	æþele trēowe.	xx/S̲sx::S̲x/Sx	xC::SA

Æsc biþ oferhēah,	eldum dȳre,	S̲x/S̲s::S̲x/Sx	SA::SA
stīþ on staþule;	stede rihte hylt,	S̲x/S̲x::S̲/Sxs	SA::SB
ðēah him feohtan on	fīras monige.	xx/S̲xs::S̲x/Sx	xB::SA

Ȳr byþ æþelinga	and eorla gehwæs	S̲x/S̲sx::x/S̲xxs	SC::xB
85 wyn and wyrþmynd;	byþ on wicge fæger,	S̲x/S̲s::xx/S̲xs	SA::xB
fæstlīc on færelde,	fyrdgeatewa sum.	S̲s/(x)S̲x::S̲sx/S	SA::CsS

Īar byþ ēafixa;	and ðēah ā brūceþ	S̲x/S̲sx::xx/S̲sx	SC::xC
fōdres on foldan;	hafaþ fægerne eard,	S̲x/(x)S̲x::s/S̲xs	SA::sB
wætre beworpen,	ðǣr hē wynnum leofaþ.	S̲x/(x)S̲x::xx/S̲xs	SA::xB

90 Ēar byþ egle	eorla gehwylcun,	S̲x/S̲x::S̲x/(x)Sx	SA::SA
ðonn fæstlīce	flǣsc onginneþ	x/S̲sx::S̲x/Sx	xC::SA
hrāw cōlian,	hrūsan cēosan	S̲/S̲xx::S̲x/S̲x	SC::SA

blāc tō gebeddan;	blēda gedrēosaþ,	S̲x̲/(x)S̲x̲::S̲x̲/(x)Sx	SA::SA
94 wynna gewītaþ,	wēra geswīcaþ.	S̲x̲/(x)S̲x̲::S̲x̲/(x)Sx	SA::SA

The Text, Scansion, and Translation of My New Stanzas

Here I present my innovated stanzas along with their scansion according to the system of Bredehoft and a literal translation. I have given my stanzas line numbers as though they were a continuation of the original poem. I have indicated the presence of palatalization in c and g by putting dots over them, ċ and ġ, where applicable.

Vocabulary notes are in order. First, I have more or less used dictionary forms of Old English words, which tend to be classical West Saxon. Halsall concludes that the text "shows only southern and basically late West Saxon forms" without any hard evidence of an early Anglian origin as others have assumed (30). I have not made a serious attempt to reproduce all peculiarities of dialect and spelling as seen in the original poem's text, though I did go for some low-hanging fruit, such as using *byþ* instead of *biþ* just as the text did in most cases. I coined a simplex word, made a loanword, and coined a few compounds that are not found in dictionaries. The latter are easily identified in my stanzas by their internal hyphens. All the roots used in my compounds are found in dictionaries. Also, the enigmatic *cweorð* deserves some comments. I will briefly remark on their definitions now.

- *bǣr-fǣġe*: an adjective meaning 'doomed to end up on a (funeral) bier.' Modeled after *dēaþfǣġe*, which simply means 'death-doomed.' Declined as strong masculine accusative singular in line 96b.

- *cweorð*: here, a feminine noun, as I am using *hēo* as the personal pronoun for it. (That would be its gender if it indeed came from **kwerþrō*.) It has a primary meaning of 'fire-drill,' but my stanza intentionally conflates it with the need-fire that it is used to produce. Used in line 95a.

- *cwica*: a masculine agent noun meaning 'quickener,' formed from the verb *cwician*, much as the noun *boda* is formed from the verb *bodian*. Used in the nominative singular in line 95b.

- *drȳ-wiga*: a masculine noun meaning 'sorcerer,' based on *drȳman*. More elaborately, it could be seen as meaning 'a magical hero or warrior.' Used in the nominative singular in line 106b. I coined it to put exceptional tertiary subordinated alliteration in that verse.

- *grāl*: a loanword masculine noun meaning 'grail,' based on the Old French *graal*. The word may have originally meant a dish, but here I am treating as something much removed from that, namely the object of a spiritual quest. Used in the nominative singular in lines 101b, 105b, and 109b. I treat this noun as part of the ordinary strong masculine declension, just as *calc*, *stān*, and *gār* are, although no oblique forms are used here.

- *gum-dōm*: a masculine noun meaning 'the authority, sovereignty, or dignity of a man.' Modeled on words like *dryhtendōm*, *earldōm*, *ealdordōm*, and *gumrīċe*. Used in the nominative singular in line 106a, and coined for the special alliteration in that line.

- *līf-ġifende*: an adjective simply meaning 'life-giving.' Declined as strong neuter nominative singular in line 105a.

- *stede-bletsung*: a feminine noun meaning either a 'blessing that consecrates a place' or 'a firmly secure blessing or consecration.' Used in the nominative singular in line 102b.

- *weġ-winn*: a neuter noun meaning 'gain or profit from the road or on a journey.' Used in the nominative singular in line 101a. I coined it for the exceptional poetics of the line.

Before the text of the stanzas themselves, here are some notes on the exceptional poetics I have used. Cweorð has no exceptional poetics. To kick off the stanza for Calc in line 98, I have used primary and secondary alliteration akin to that found in line 36 of the original poem. I have ended the Calc stanza with a rare quadruple alliteration in line 101. Stān features ordinary secondary alliteration in its last two lines, 104–05. Finally, the stanza for Gār starts in line 106 with a dense primary and secondary alliteration similar to line 36 of the original poem, but further packed with an unprecedented, but highly subordinated, tertiary alliteration in the b-verse. The Gār stanza also features three strongly parallel half lines

271

with weak syllable rhymes, 107a–08a, which are meant to recall those that end the Ēar stanza.

My literal translation of these stanzas follows immediately after the Old English given here. For the modern English poetic translations of these stanzas, see my discussion in the next section of this essay — I have appended them to my poetic translation of the complete original OERP.

Finally, as before, primary alliteration is indicated with underline and secondary alliteration is indicated with double underline (found only in lines 98, 104, 105, and 106). The exceptional tertiary alliteration in line 106 is indicated with underdot (ṣ).

95	Cweorð byþ cweorna sum	and se cwica fȳres;	Sx/Sxs::xx/Ssx	SB::xC
	bēam hēo byrneð,	bær-fǣġne þeġn;	Sx/Sx::Ssx/S	SA::CsS
	sāwle hēo lȳseð,	þe sēċeð rodor.	Sx/(x)Sx::x/Sxs	SA::xB
	Calc byþ cūþ wel	cēnum wōðborum	Sx/Ss::Sx/Ssx	SA::SC
	swā se hālga horn,	hefiġ mid lēoðum,	xx/Sxs::Sx/Sx	xB::SA
100	nȳdfull æt symble;	þes naca dweorga,	Sx/(x)Sx::x/Ssx	SA::xC
	weġ-winn Wōdnes,	byþ wynsum grāl.	Ss/Sx::x/Sxs	SA::xB
	Stān byþ strangest	swā stede-bletsung	Sx/Sx::x/Ssx	SA::xC
	ġif ġehālgod write,	hǣðenum rūnum:	xx/Sxs::Sxx/Sx	xB::SA
	hearga ǣċe;	þēos heorte eotenes,	Sx/Sx::(x)Sx/Sx	SA::SA
105	līf-ġifende tācn,	byþ langsum grāl.	Ssx/S::x/Sxs	CsS::xB
	Gār byþ gum-dōm,	gūðwuda drȳ-wiga:	Sx/Ss::Ss/Ssx	SA::SC
	wyrde hē wealdeð,	wæl hē ċēoseð,	Sx/(x)Sx::Sx/Sx	SA::SA
	blōd hē bēodeð;	þes brand Wōdnes,	Sx/Sx::x/Ssx	SA::xC
109	unġemetum ēaċen,	byþ æðele grāl.	Sxxx/Sx::x/Sxs	SA::xB

- *Querth* is a sort of quern and the quickener of fire. It burns a tree, a thane doomed to the bier. It releases a soul, which seeks the heavens.

- *Cup* is known well by keen bearers of inspiration and madness as the holy horn, heavy with poems and necessary at sumbel. This boat of dwarves, a journey-gain of Woden, is a winsome grail.

- *Stone* is strongest as a blessing for a place if hallowed with writing, with heathen runes: an eternal altar. This heart of the etin, a life-giving sign, is an enduring grail.

- *Spear* is man's sovereignty and a sorcerous hero of battle-woods. It rules over wyrd, it chooses the slain, it summons blood. This fiery brand of Woden, immeasurably powerful, is a noble grail.

My Poetic Translation of the OERP with My Extension

I have also made a translation of the OERP into the modern alliterative meter that I use. Since having a poetic translation was my highest priority here, I have occasionally sacrificed the literal meaning of the words, but hopefully in a manner that preserves the spirit of the original. As a Runer myself, it will hopefully be friendly and useful to other Runers as well. Also, I have appended translations of my innovated stanzas for Cweorð, Calc, Stān, and Gār to the end as I consider them a continuation of the poem. The translated rune names are in bold.

Some remarks on my translation and its meter are in order here. No scansion is provided, as my own system is still being developed, and it is not necessarily a word-foot system as the Old English one was. I do, however, use a long line that is broken up into a pair of half lines. Usually each half line will have two significant stresses, and at least one stress in the first half line must alliterate with the first stress in the second half line. Beyond that, I tend to use secondary alliteration much more than the OERP poet. I have implemented hypermetric lines as having three distinct significant stresses, and I have loaded them with secondary alliteration. I use them in the same places that the OERP poet used them: the Hail and Need stanzas. I also preserved the line count for each stanza. Where the OERP poet used three lines, I have also used three lines, and so forth.

Note that this translation does not always go line-by-line. In order to keep the meter, concepts were swapped between half lines or even long lines as needed. For example, my translation of the Ēþel

273

stanza into the Estate stanza has very much reordered what was present in the original lines in order to make it intelligible and poetic at the same time.

As with my innovated Old English stanzas, some vocabulary notes are in order. I have not coined any compounds that need explaining here, but I have used some loanwords, many of which are proper names.

- *drighten*: a loanword noun of Old English *dryhten*, commonly meaning 'lord' or 'leader of a war-band.' The Anglo-Saxons frequently used this word for the Christian deity. Used in the Fee, Man, and Day stanzas.

- *Heardings*: a loanword proper noun from Old English *heardingas*. It also means 'warriors' and is usually translated that way. Halsall notes that Dickins treats it as the name of a tribe, connected to Old Norse Haddingjar (148). I chose to concur with Dickins here. Used in the Ing stanza.

- *Ing*: a loanword proper noun. I treated this as the name of an Old English mythological hero or god, just like everyone else. It is too bad we do not have more Old English sources about him. Used in the Ing stanza.

- *ose*: a loanword noun of Old English *ōs*, meaning 'a heathen god.' Taken from Edred (*Alu* 41). I could have translated it as simply 'god,' and I think the OERP poet meant it as that primarily while also being a pun on a Latin word for 'mouth,' though *ōs* is never used by anyone else to refer to the Christian deity, which is probably who he meant. Translating as 'god' would come off as too Christian for my purposes, but coming out and naming Woden directly did not seem quite right here either. Used in the Ose stanza.

- *Perth*: a loanword proper noun. Halsall considers this might have been the name of a game (128). This was also the interpretation I had before reading her text, and I am sticking with it. Used in the Perth stanza.

- *querth*: a loanword noun. I could have used fire-drill, given the meaning that I am working with, but I did not want to pin it down that much as I am also conflating it with the need-fire that it is used to create. Used in the Querth stanza.

- *Tir*: a loanword proper noun. Some translate this as 'glory,' which is what it means as a common noun. Halsall sees it as the name of a star or other heavenly object (135). I concur with Halsall. Used in the Tir stanza.

- *wode-bearer*: a loan word of Old English *wōðbora*. Not merely a poet, but perhaps also a sage and philosopher. Possibly an ecstatic professional of early Germanic society. See Hollowell's article for further details. Here, I particularly mean a bearer of *wode*. *Wode*, as I use it here, is a word meaning poetry, creativity, inspiration, madness, ecstasy, fury, and potentially other related ideas all rolled into one. Used in the Cup stanza.

- *Woden*: a loanword proper noun from Old English *Wōden*. I could have used 'Óðinn' and that would have been more familiar to my readers, but this particular project is rooted in the English tradition, and so sticking with an originally English form seemed best. Used in the Cup (where it alliterates better than 'Óðinn' would) and Gar stanzas.

Finally, some brief notes on exceptional poetics. In the third line of the Torch stanza, I treat *on* as a stressed word and a participant in the alliteration, which is quite rare for it. The last three half-lines of the Grave stanza attempt to reproduce some of the parallelism, matching rhythms, and unstressed syllable rhymes of their counterparts in the original poem. Three half-lines in my stanza for Gar attempt to reproduce a strong parallelism present in the Old English. Since I use secondary alliteration much more frequently than the OERP poet, one should not read too much into its presence or absence in a particular line. [*The poem is titled "New Old English Rune Poem" and may be found in the Rune-Work Poems chapter.*]

275

An Esoteric Analysis of My New Stanzas

Here I present an esoteric analysis of my innovated stanzas. As the basis of the analysis, I conducted Rune-Thinking exercises with the stanzas as described by Edred in the Fourth Door of Midgard (*Nine* 90). I contemplated the Old English that I composed, not my poetic or literal translations. Thus, some of the aspects I mention here may be things that were lost in the translations. Some of what is mentioned here are things that I intentionally put into the stanzas, but other things were delightful discoveries that I only found when doing the Rune-Thinking.

Cweorð is thematically connected with the Ēar stanza preceding it as a means of disposing of a corpse, but while Ēar is the path of decay into the ground, Cweorð provides the alternative of incineration for sending the soul into the sky. Its position after Ēar suggests that one must in some way first embrace death (that is, significant change or transformation) in order to be in a state where the querth can set one on fire. Thus the opportunity to overcome the grave is presented as one that first requires it. However, this path is not open to just anyone, as the use of the word *þegn*, 'thane,' indicates a connection to nobles or the elite, as nearly any single-syllable word for 'man' could have been used in that spot without affecting the meter.

In this stanza, Cweorð is a tool for creating a need-fire and it is also conflated with the fire that it makes, especially when used for the above-mentioned cremation. Thus, it is a need-fire that burns the one who makes it in order to cause self-transformation. This transformation is the means to freedom for the soul. It spurs the soul on the journey to immortality, as indicated by the word *rodor*, which especially denotes the firmament containing the fixed and permanent stars — it is the goal of the initiate to attain such a permanent nature.

The presence of three active verbs in the stanza (*byrneð, lȳseð, sēceð*; 'burns,' 'releases,' 'seeks'), an unusually high number for the OERP, suggests that this is a rune that requires action by the would-be initiate, and the verbs themselves tell us what he needs to do. The phrase *cweorna sum* emphasizes the grinding and turning aspects of this action. A quern is a mill turned by hand, by the power of its user. Thus a querth must also be turned by its user — it cannot be hooked up to a stream or waterfall to turn it. (If he is not careful, the turning can wear the user down instead!) Alternatively, a quern grinds grain into meal; by analogy, the querth takes in tinder and produces fire, or it takes in gross matter and produces the release of the trapped soul. As a quickener, it gives life to the inner fire of the soul. Being located in the fourth *ætt* right under Ing is perhaps a subtle indication that this is a fire that needs to be lit under the would-be hero!

The repeated presence of the feminine personal pronoun *hēo*, 'she,' provides a doorway for the fetch to enter into this stanza, which is seen as female in form for the male seeker. (The sexes may be varied appropriately according to the sex and sexual preference of the seeker, but a poem like this cannot accommodate an awkward he/she sequence.) So on one level it is the Cweorð that burns and releases the individual, but on another level it may be the fetch that does this. The connection is strengthened by the numerology: Cweorð is stave 30 in the row and thus a significant doubling of stave 15, Eolhx, which is strongly associated with the fetch.

The b-alliteration in the second line connects it to Beorc, and thus ideas of new growth in spite of apparent sterility, especially as might result from burning. The s-alliteration in the third line connects it to Siġel, which refers to the guiding aspects of the sun to keep one on proper course and heading toward the goal. In the case of Cweorð, that goal is initiation: *þe sēċeð rodor*, 'which seeks the heavens.'

In the Gild's system, we can connect it to the work of the Associate, for it is the task of the Associate to ignite an inner fire of passion for the seeking of Rûna and having a Rûna Experience. His own efforts must turn the querth within to produce that flame. Lastly, it should be noted that Cweorð quickens fire (*cwica fȳres*), but that Ēoh keeps fire (*hyrde fȳres*). A mystery is hidden here.

Calc is by its shape most obviously connected to Eolhx, which occurs two *ættir* above it in the Fuþorc. This is most appropriate, as it is the valkyrie or fetch that is usually depicted bringing the mead cup to the hero. Thus once the inner fire is kindled by Cweorð, a drink from the chalice comes next. This cup is identified as the Germanic drinking horn and the "drunkenness" of inspiration that leads to songs and poems. The horn, described as holy, implies a wholeness and right order. It also contains notions of fellowship implied by the statement that it is 'necessary at sumbel,' the Germanic ritual drinking celebration. The *wōðborum*, who are something much more than ordinary poets, must know this rune especially well. The use of *cēnum* in the first line to describe the *wōðborum* indicates some properties of the drink and its archetypal drinkers: keen, fierce, bold, brave, warlike — all of which are manifestations of *wode* when properly channeled.

In the lines *þes naca dweorga, weġ-winn Wōdnes*, the sumbel horn is linked with the corresponding mythological object: Óðrœrir, the stirrer of poetry. From this and what has come before, Calc is very strongly linked with poetry itself. As 'boat of dwarves,' we are reminded that poetry can function as a currency for buying certain things. It ransomed those dwarves from Suttung, and it ransomed Egill's head from King Eirik Bloodaxe. Buying one's life is simply one of the most extreme examples of poetry functioning as money. Thus, in the best poetry, words are made concrete and can circulate as mobile power. That mobile power is like Feoh and should be dealt out like it as well: the poet must pour out his poetry. 'Boat of dwarves' also indicates that the Calc should also be thought of as a means of transportation as well — in this case, it moves our spirits, as anyone hearing extremely good poetry can attest. As a 'journey gain of Woden,' we are reminded that we must quest for it, just as he did. It will not come to us if we do not seek it. This quest involved his sexual relations with an etin woman — more echoes of interaction with one's valkyrie or fetch in the process of gaining Calc.

The final phrase, *wynsum grāl*, identifies it as one of the grails and thus the object of a spiritual quest. The adjective identifies it as something that is winsome, pleasant, and joyful to have — more echoes of the conviviality of a sumbel and the happiness from its attainment. As indicated in the mythological discussion, it is a grail that is won through a quest, as Óðinn won the mead through a quest. (As will be seen, the other grails are won in different ways.)

The alliterations make connections to several other runes. The secondary w-alliteration in the first line and the primary quadruple w-alliteration in the last line connect it to Wynn, which is also named as part of the word *wynsum*. Joy is thus an essential aspect of this stave, and one who seeks Calc should follow the advice of that stanza. The n-alliteration of the third line connects it to Nȳd, which is also named as part of the word *nȳdfull*. The Calc may be a burden or hardship at times, but it is essential and one should heed it to gain the help and salvation spoken about in the Nȳd stanza — this is reinforced by its description as heavy, which may also indicate the intensity of the flow of inspiration. The second line h-alliteration connects it to Hæġl. Here we can see Calc as the seed of poetry and inspiration — its often temporary nature is hinted at also. Sudden and intense, such an ecstatic episode can be over all too quickly, just like the hail. It is stave 31, which is prime, making it unique and isolated. This is quite appropriate, as the transformative power of the mead makes one set apart and sacred.

In the Gild's system, we can connect it to the work of the Learner, for it is his task, having lit the transformative fire to seek out inspiration and maintain it, through his further readings and exercises and to ultimately demonstrate this inspiration in a Fellow Work.

Ritually, the contents of a cup are poured out upon a stone in a heathen blessing. (See the *Hyndluljóð*, where Óttar is said to have reddened a rock altar with blood and thus gained the favor of the goddess Freyja, who can perhaps be seen as acting in the role of his fetch in that poem.) Herein lies a Rune: namely, the Runer should seek to pour his inspiration out upon his immortal core of Self. There will be more about this in the discussion of Stān.

279

Stān is the last rune in the fourth *ætt* and is thus in a sense the summation of the runes, hence the mention of runes being carved on it. (Here, I regard Gār as perhaps being outside of the *ætt* system.) It is connected quite significantly to Siġel by its sound. The numerology reinforces this: as stave 32 it is a significant doubling of Siġel, stave 16. Indeed, both are guides and beacons. In the sky, the sun provides light and direction, allowing a traveller to orient himself. On the ground, stones were often way-markers for travelers, and a stone carved with runes is a beacon. For those who can read them, such stones often commemorated the dead, keeping their memory alive, a sort of immortality. Whether readable or not, they represented a source of mystery as well. Stone serves as a focal point for energies and mental attention: as a dense, hard material it can do this better than wood or other perishable materials. That is an essential attribute for Stān as a 'stead-blessing': a blessing that is firm and secure and a blessing that is on a particular place. 'If hallowed with writing' indicates the power of stone is best used when we impress our will upon it, and the 'heathen runes' — *mysteries* — are the most powerful and effective things we can carve into stone. (The combining of *ġehālgod* and *hǣðenum* in this fashion would have been shocking to the Christian Anglo-Saxons, but it also helps capture the synthesis of opposites that is part of the mystery of Stān, as it is between Calc and Gār.) The stone itself is thus rendered an 'eternal altar' through such important work.

An essential clue to the work of the rune-seeker is thus given here: the initiate must 'hallow' with runes the most permanent and stone-like part of himself (and he may first have to create this medium) in order to be transformed into an 'eternal altar.' (By the way, that permanent part is not the physical body, so do not rush out and get runic tattoos on account of this!)

In the lines *þēos heorte eotenes, līf-ġifende tācn*, the hallowed stone is linked with the corresponding mythological object: the 'heart of the etin,' which here means Hrungnir's heart, the stone *par excellence* which Thor wins for the gods though his duel with Hrungnir. This heart may also be the valknut. As life-giving, it is

280

identified as something that provides immortality just as Wolfram's grail is described as prolonging life. Some clues to the mystery of immortality and life after death are thus found here in the valknut and Hrungnir's heart.

The final phrase, *langsum grāl*, identifies it as one of the grails and thus the object of a spiritual quest. The adjective identifies it as something that is enduring, lasting, and permanent — but it is something that takes a long time as well, indicating that this is a grail that cannot be gained in short order. As indicated in the mythological discussion, it is a grail that is won through a battle. This also parallels the situation of Wolfram's *Parzival* who is said to have attained the grail through fighting, although this is considered exceptional (334). For the would-be initiate, the essential battle is within.

The alliterative connections are interesting as well. The secondary vowel-alliteration in the third line connects it to notions of the World Tree and its permanence, especially since the alliterating staves are Æsc and Ēoh, the two species most closely connected to the World Tree. The h-alliteration in lines two and three connects it with Hæġl. Stone is in some sense hail transformed: the tiny seed of temporary duration has become a hard lump of permanent duration. The l-alliteration in the fourth line links it to Lagu. This is perhaps reminiscent of the liquid from a cup that is poured onto a stone in a heathen ritual. (See also the discussion of Calc.) The secondary mixed ġ/g-alliteration (and the use of a Ġyfu derivative) in the same line perhaps anticipates one possible purpose: by pouring gifts upon the stone, the way is made toward gaining Gār, and that line indeed immediately precedes the Gār stanza. Although it is very subtle and not an alliteration, the anacrusis in the third line (104b) provides a link to the only other instance of anacrusis in the OERP, line 11b in the Ōs stanza. We should thus ponder whether the heart of the etin is also *witena frōfur*, 'a comfort to wizards.'

Beyond its connection with Siġel, the numerology of Stān connects it to a few more things. Four is "stasis, solidity, and waiting" and it holds power; eight is "complete manifestation of

281

wholeness and perfect symmetry" (*Runelore* 162-63). Thus Stān as stave 32 (4 x 8) is the perfect synthesis of both these sets of qualities over all directions. Also, its sum is five and thus notions of "ordered time and space" (*Runelore* 162). All of this fits Stān quite well in many ways.

In the Gild's system, we can connect it to the work of the Fellow, for it is his task, with the transformative fire and the mead of inspiration, to gain a permanent core essence: something that will survive the transformation known as death. The Master Work will show evidence of this permanence, among other things.

Gār is reckoned as the ninth rune of the fourth *ætt*, the first rune of a fifth *ætt*, or as totally outside the *ætt* system. In any case, it is exceptional, and so is its stanza, which is all about power and action. *Gum-dōm*, 'sovereignty of a man' recalls the role of the spear as a sign of the manhood and voting rights of the Germanic tribesman. The next phrase, *gūðwuda drȳ-wiga*, is complex. *Gūðwuda*, 'of war-woods,' is a word for spear, but can also be a kenning for warrior via the identification of humans with trees. *Drȳ-wiga* is 'a sorcerous hero.' Thus the *gūðwuda drȳ-wiga* is a magical hero of warriors who is a cut above the regular warriors. This in addition to the phrase identifying the spear as a war-wood above others because of its sorcerous nature as revealed in the next three half-lines. Esoterically, these ideas suggest the completed initiate who has risen above the ordinary.

The parallel phrases and unstressed syllable rhymes in lines 107a–08a recall the ending of the Ēar stanza, suggesting that this is now the new end of the poem — that this Gār is the ultimate end for the initiated, whereas the grave is the ultimate end for the uninitiated. Thus, these three half lines with their active verbs deserve a close and careful look. First, it is noted that the use of the masculine personal pronoun, *hē*, 'he,' provides a doorway for the wode-self to enter into this stanza, which is seen as male in form for the male seeker. This recalls the discussion of Cweorð and the possibility for the fetch in it. Since the Gild sees the fetch and wode-self as a pair, the completion of the pair in this stanza suggests that

Gār is the completion of what was started in Cweorð. In any case, in the highest forms of rune-magic, it is the wode-self that exercises the powers of Gār. Put another way, one who has truly attained Gār has surely attained his wode-self as well.

Now for a look at the spear's powers, as indicated by the three active verbs: rulership, choice, and summoning/proclaiming. *Wyrde hē wealdeð*: this is the spear of destiny, for it rules over wyrd and can thus change it. (*Wyrd* can mean 'what happens': thus the spear affects chance, fortune, and the ordaining of events.) *Wæl hē ċeoseð*: this is an Odinic power, choosing the slain and hallowing them to death so that they are given to the other world. The spear chooses who lives and who dies. At a higher level, this is the power to hallow someone as one of the Einherjar. *Blōd hē bēodeð*: it causes blood to flow from wounds, but it is more than that. At a higher level, it calls to the blood of Óðinn's Folk, summoning individuals to return to the elder troth of their ancestors. It indicates the mystery of sacral kingship and the power to legitimately govern the Folk. It is also the royal scepter as a symbol of the authority and divine descent of the king.

In the lines *þes brand Wōdnes, unġemetum ēaċen*, this spear of destiny is linked with the corresponding mythological object: Gungnir, the spear of Óðinn, which was forged by dwarves and delivered by Loki. 'Brand' indicates its fiery and flaming nature, connecting it to its Celtic and Grail mythos counterparts. We might see this as the glow of charisma or authority, and it also reinforces the notion of the spear as a summoning beacon in the preceding half line. Although not mentioned in the stanza, we are reminded that Óðinn was wounded with a spear when hanging on the World Tree to win the Runes and that he cast a spear over the opposing army at the start of the first war. (Considering the position of Gār in the Fuþorc, we thus have the suggestion that the runes "end" at the same place they began.) The 'immeasurably powerful' nature of it reminds us of the Dolorous Stroke associated with the spear in the Grail Mythos when someone who was unworthy picked it up and used it. Furthermore, 'immeasurably powerful' suggests that as the hammer

283

is the ultimate symbol of Thoric power, the spear is the ultimate symbol of Odinic power.

The final phrase, *æðele grāl*, identifies it as one of the grails and thus the object of a spiritual quest. The adjective identifies it as something that is associated with excellence, the nobility, the elite, and thus Dumézil's first function. One who achieves it is very much set apart. Gungnir was said to never stop in its thrust, suggesting that the one who attains this grail has reached a level of permanent action and activity, which is reminiscent of the Einherjar of Valhalla. The mythology of Gungnir's origin suggests that one wins this grail by forging it through hard work with the agency of one's shadow self.

Now I look at the alliterative connections. The extremely exceptional first line alliteration indicates the powers of Dæġ and Wynn as most essential to the mastery of Gār. He who would have Gār must first radiate day like a drighten and possess a hidden joy within. The unusual b-verse alliteration may also indicate a power to break the rules and thus transcend ordinary reality. The rest of the stanza contains no exceptional alliteration. The w-alliteration in the second line (manifest instead of hidden) reinforces the connection to Wynn, reiterating the theme of joy that is a constant undercurrent in the OERP. The b-alliteration of the third line connects it to Beorc, and its nature as isolated (on account of its fruitlessness), tall, and touching the sky may be most appropriate here. The vowel-alliteration in the final line makes no obvious pattern, but links to the runes Ūr, Ēar, and Æsc: a mystery may or may not be hidden here. In Stān, the vowel-alliteration pointed to the World Tree in particular. However, might any vowel-alliteration be seen as esoterically linked to the vertical column of the World Tree, at least in the Gild's system which uses vowels for the worlds in the Yew Work?

Its numerology is fairly straightforward. As stave 33, it is 3 x 11 and is thus a significant tripling of Īs, suggesting the very high level of focus and solidity needed for the power of Gār. Three is also the number of Þorn, and we may note one of the key words in this stanza, *ungemetum*, is found in both the Þorn and Īs stanzas and nowhere else in the poem. This may suggest that Gār is a treasure like Īs (*ġimmum ġelīcust*) though it is sharp like Þorn (*þearle scearp*). Both Þorn and Īs are dangerous, suggesting that Gār is even more so. The Þorn connection also recalls the Dolorous Stroke mentioned above.

In the Gild's system, we can connect it to the work of the Master. It is his task, having completed the other grails, to now teach and *act* in the world. The Master Work shows what the nature of that teaching and acting is likely to be. Gār is thus a guide to the nature and power of the action that is aimed at. As a final note, the power of Gār can perhaps be seen as the "tree" that grows when the Calc of inspiration is poured out upon the Stān of self.

Finally, I make some brief comments on the three grails together. From the stanza endings, we see that the significant attributes of the grails are joy, permanence, and nobility, and the initiate must gain these qualities as well. Connecting them to the cosmology, we can see Calc as the Well, Gār as the Tree, and Stān as the middle-point meeting place of Midgard. Stone is, after all, the most permanent and the most fundamental material from which the earth is made. The surface of our world changes much and has variety, but go underground far enough, and it is nothing but stone all the rest of the way down. Thus the initiate's attaining a permanent nature is essential to completing the cycle and allowing a vivifying and dynamic flow between the Well of Calc and the Tree of Gār. For now, further commentary on the interactions between the grails will have to await future work.

Conclusion

There is no denying that the Grail Mythos has a quite an appeal, even today after all these centuries. It fascinates us immensely. It is an initiatory mythos, one that is quite well developed in Wolfram's *Parzival*. His is Christianized, but certainly not orthodox — even if we do not wish to go as far as Edred in claiming that there really is nothing Christian about the original Grail Mythos (*Alu* 206). There is great power in it to move people and nations. This is a power that the modern Heathen Germanic revival can make use of, but it will first be necessary to remove the Christian overlays and replace it with what is Heathen. The presence of the Grail Mythos in the Anglo-Saxon Fuþorc is a doorway for this work, and I have chosen to follow Edred in stepping through it. I hope my work here has made this doorway wider for those who will follow in the future.

Those who value the use of poetic stanzas in their magical and divinatory rune-work now have a powerful tool by which their work with the runes of Cweorð, Calc, Stān, and Gār can be made much more effective. Others may wish to try them in Rune-Thinking exercises as I have. Some may even take up the challenge to compose alternate stanzas in Old English. Many further mysteries can perhaps be discovered from the stanzas if I have indeed filled them with objective seeds instead of my own personal whims. Some in the Gild already connect the Grail Runes to the steps of its initiatory model, and I hope that my contribution can help develop that approach, for it is one which I wholly support. Other possibilities include ritual use, as the grail stories of Chrétien and Wolfram both include grail processions. A ritual that includes reciting the stanzas could be developed based on those processions. Regardless of what others do with the stanzas, I myself now have a very powerful tool for my further explorations of the Grail Mysteries.

In the farther future, the runic revival will eventually suggest the possibility of producing a modern English Fuþorc, reformed and updated for the modern language, just as the old Fuþarks were reformed and updated for their languages. Edred has offered an interesting beginning to this work in a system of modern English names for the thirty-three staves (*Alu* 41). More work will be needed in the future (those names will need poetic stanzas eventually, among other things), and perhaps my own efforts here can help further that work by fleshing out the foundation that it will start from. *Reyn til Rúna!*

Works Cited

Beowulf = *Klaeber's Beowulf.* Eds. R. D. Fulk, Robert E. Bjork, and John D. Niles. 4th ed. Toronto: U of Toronto P, 2008. Print.

Bredehoft, Thomas A. *Early English Metre.* Toronto: U of Toronto P, 2005. Print.

Brown, Arthur C. L. "The Bleeding Lance." *Publications of the Modern Language Association.* 25.1 (1910): 1–59. Print.

Chrétien de Troyes. *The Complete Romances of Chrétien de Troyes.* Trans. David Staines. Bloomington: Indiana UP, 1990. Print.

Edred Thorsson. *Alu: An Advanced Guide to Operative Runology.* San Francisco: Weiser, 2012. Print.

———. *The Nine Doors of Midgard.* 5th ed. The Rune-Gild, 2016. Print.

———. *Runelore.* York Beach: Weiser, 1987. Print.

Eliade, Mircea. *A History of Religious Ideas.* Vol. 3. Trans. Alf Hiltebeitel and Diane Apostolos-Cappadona. Chicago: U of Chicago P, 1985. Print.

Halsall, Maureen. *The Old English Rune Poem: A Critical Edition.* Toronto: U of Toronto P, 1981. Print.

Hollowell, Ida Masters. "*Scop* and *Woðbora* in OE Poetry." *The Journal of English and Germanic Philology.* 77.3 (July 1978): 317–29. Print.

Jones, Frederick George, Jr. "The Old English Rune Poem, an Edition." Diss. U of Florida, 1967. Print.

Murphy, G. Ronald. *Gemstone of Paradise: The Holy Grail in Wolfram's Parzival.* Oxford: Oxford UP, 2006. Print.

Puhvel, Jaan. *Comparative Mythology.* Baltimore: Johns Hopkins UP, 1987. Print.

Ravenscroft, Trevor. *The Spear of Destiny.* York Beach: Weiser, 1973. Print.

Simek, Rudolf. *Dictionary of Northern Mythology*. Trans. Angela Hall. Cambridge: D.S. Brewer, 1993. Print.

Snorri Sturluson. *Edda*. Trans. Anthony Faulkes. London: Everyman, 1987. Print.

Wolfram von Eschenbach. *Parzival and Titurel*. Trans. Cyril Edwards. Oxford: Oxford UP, 2006. Print.

Ynglinga saga = Snorri Sturluson. *Ynglinga saga*. In *Heimskringla*, vol. 1, trans. Alison Finaly and Anthony Faulkes, 6–47. London: Viking Society for Northern Research, 2011.

Additional Selected Bibliography

Alaric Albertsson. *Wydworking: The Path of a Saxon Sorcerer*. Woodbury: Llewellyn P, 2011. Print.

Bosworth, Joseph. "An Anglo-Saxon Dictionary Online." Ed. Thomas Northcote Toller, et al. Comp. Sean Christ and Ondřej Tichý. Faculty of Arts, Charles University in Prague. Web. <http://www.bosworthtoller.com/>.

Clark-Hall, J. R. *A Concise Anglo-Saxon Dictionary*. 2nd ed. New York: The Macmillan Company, 1916. Print.

Edred Thorsson. "Anglo-Saxon Runes." *Radio Free Rúna*, Episode 3x05. Austin: Edred.net, 2011. Audio.

———. "Calc, Stan, and Gar." *Radio Free Rúna*, Episode 2x06. Austin: Edred.net, 2010. Audio.

———. *Rune-Song*. Austin: Runa-Raven Press, 1993. Print and CD.

Elliott, Ralph W. V. *Runes: An Introduction*. 2nd ed. Manchester: Manchester UP, 1989. Print.

Flowers, Stephen. *Black Rûna*. Austin: Runa-Raven Press, 1995. Print.

———. "Old English Rune Poem." *Woodharrow Lecture Series*. June 8, 2008. Audio.

————. *The Rune-Poems*. Vol. 1. Austin: Runa-Raven Press, 2002. Print.

Hall, J. R. "Perspective and Wordplay in the Old English Rune Poem." *Neophilologus*. 61.3 (July 1977): 453–60. Print.

Millar, Angel. "The Old English Rune Poem — Semantics, Structure, and Symmetry." *The Journal of Indo-European Studies*. 34.3/4 (Fall/Winter 2006): 419–36. Print.

Page, R. I. *An Introduction to English Runes*. 2nd ed. Woodbridge. The Boydell P, 1999. Print.

Pollington, Stephen. *Rudiments of Runelore*. Norfolk: Anglo-Saxon Books, 1995. Print.

Russom, Geoffrey. *Beowulf and Old Germanic Metre*. Cambridge: Cambridge UP, 1998. Print.

————. *Old English Meter and Linguistic Theory*. Cambridge: Cambridge UP, 1987. Print.

Wódening, Eric. *The Old English Rune Poem: Translation and Interpretation*. 2nd ed. Baltimore: White Marsh P, 2011. Print.

Whom Does (the Story of) the Grail Serve? The Chivalric Ideals Communicated in Chrétien's Romances.

Introduction

Chrétien's romances provide a guide to knightly behavior — Keen notes that "their heroes presented a model of true chivalry" (2). Compared to the first four romances, the final, unfinished romance, *The Story of the Grail*, is different. It starts with an unlikely hero. It gives a much larger role to Gawain. It does not focus on the usual knightly quest to win the love of a woman. Pickens says: "No other work by Chrétien is so infused with religious sentiment and doctrine" (171). This essay first briefly explores what knightly ideals are being communicated in each of the first four romances. Zink points out that Chrétien indicated the meanings of the romances in their prologues (56). Thus in looking for their knightly ideals, I will include a consideration of those prologues. Then I will take a more in-depth look at what ideal is being communicated by *The Story of the Grail* and how it differs from the others. I will show that *The Story of the Grail* is indeed different in that it is about knighthood itself in a way that the others are not, and that it has a more serious mission compared to the others.

The Ideals in the First Four Romances

I begin by considering the main ideals of chivalry shown in each of the first four romances. These ideals are primarily shown through the heroes of each romance: Erec (and Enide), Cligès (and his father Alexander), Lancelot, and Yvain. Chrétien tells us about each ideal in his prologues — sometimes directly, sometimes more obliquely. In addition, I briefly consider how the special figure of Gawain relates to the ideals discussed, since he occurs in all four romances.

In *Erec and Enide*, Chrétien opens with a proverb about properly valuing what one has and is quite direct when he says his story "clearly proves that a man does not act intelligently if he does not give free rein to his knowledge" (37). The theme behind this begins to flower when Enide lets slip her anguish at hearing the shameful things spoken about Erec due to his having abandoned knightly deeds for the comforts of love — this spurs him to resume such deeds (68–69). Also, in the romance, there are numerous instances (to the point where they become tedious) of Erec telling his wife not to warn him about whatever danger may be coming along ahead. Yet each time, Enide warns him anyway, likely saving his life. Yet Chrétien, however, has Enide say: "A good silence never harmed anyone, but speaking often causes harm!" (94). He is perhaps being tongue-in-cheek here. (On top of that, this praise of silence contradicts a very blatant theme in *The Story of the Grail*!) In the end, however, Erec and Enide's love is stronger because they appreciate each other more, and their fame is greater. Thus in this romance, the ideal seems to be that giving free rein to one's knowledge is about honest communication of what one knows, even if it is risky or one is asked not to do it, and that this leads to properly appreciating what one has.

In *Cligès*, there is a theme of seeking glory by traveling to foreign lands. Chrétien hints at this theme in the prologue, when he says of a knight that, "in order to win fame and glory, he went from Greece to England," and in which he praises old books that reveal the origins of chivalry and learning in Greece and Rome, lands that are foreign with respect to France (123). The knight is Alexander, and having such a complete upbringing that he lacks nothing in the court of his father (the emperor in Constantinople), he absolutely insists on traveling abroad to King Arthur in Britain to be knighted by him and no one else (124). He obtains this knighting and gains the glory that he seeks, as well as a wife and a son. He returns to Constantinople upon hearing of his father's death and assumes rulership in his mature state. (The complications presented by Alis do not fundamentally alter this.) Alexander, on his own deathbed, advises his son Cligès to do likewise: to travel abroad and test himself at King Arthur's court (154). Cligès takes the advice and gains glory in a foreign land and a lady as well. Cligès also ultimately returns to Constantinople, and eventually to rulership. (The complications presented by Alis delay, but do not alter, this underlying theme.) Thus the ideal displayed is that of seeking out the unfamiliar and far-off for the purpose of being tested and matured by it (through gaining glory and a lady) — but this is to be followed by a return to one's home to assume a level of rulership.

In *The Knight of the Cart*, Lancelot is absolutely devoted to Guinevere in his quest to rescue her. His devotion enables him to set aside his ego and undertake whatever action is needed, whatever the cost. This is quite a contrast with the passivity, inaction, and resignation that King Arthur displays in response to the knight who challenges him at the beginning of the romance (208). Two instances of Lancelot's devotion are most notable. First, to find out where the queen is held, he rides in the back of a cart, something that is extraordinarily shameful for a knight, since it equates him with a lowly criminal (211). His devotion is not perfect, however, as he hesitates before getting into the cart. Later, his devotion is perfect when he is anonymously fighting in a tournament. Guinevere suspects it is him, and to test this, she asks him to do his worst (277). Lancelot complies without hesitation, apparently setting aside his pride and shame completely. This devotion is mirrored in the prologue, where Chrétien says: "Since my lady of Champagne wishes me to begin a romance, I shall do so most willingly, like one who is entirely at her service in anything he can undertake in this world" (207). From those notable scenes in the romance, it is clear that the ideal displayed is that of absolute devotion to something outside of oneself, and that this can overcome any internal obstacle of the ego.

In *The Knight with the Lion*, Chrétien gives us the hint in the prologue by first telling us about Arthur, "whose valour teaches us to be brave and courteous" (295). Then he informs us that "very few serve love," referring also to "empty pleasantries" and "mockery" in regard to it. These indeed relate to Yvain's theme. He gains his lady through a deed of valour, and intends to serve love by staying with her. However, he is reminded that he cannot remain idle, and must frequent tournaments and so forth to maintain his honor (326). His lady, knowing that knights can get carried away with such things, demands that he return in a certain amount of time (327). He agrees to the condition, but instead makes a mockery of his love and fails to serve it properly by not returning within the specified time. He therefore has to spend the rest of the romance working very hard to regain his lady. Thus the ideal is to maintain one's honor, but to take care not to neglect love and one's lady at the same time — a theme of moderation and reconciliation between those two duties, which often seem opposed, just as they were juxtaposed in the prologue.

Gawain is in all four of the romances, yet in a way he stands outside all of them as well, for he is never the main character. Gawain instead is a model of knightly behavior who provides a pivotal counterpoint for others. In *Erec and Enide*, he openly warns King Arthur that the Tradition of the White Stag will cause problems (37), displaying the ideal of open communication in the first direct speech in the romance. In *Cligès*, Alexander specifically tells his son to test himself against Gawain (154), and Cligès' battle with Gawain is indeed a centerpiece of his being tested in a foreign land. In *The Knight of the Cart*, Gawain comes to the same cart that Lancelot rides in, but he refuses to get in and instead stays on his horse and follows it, highlighting the shameful behavior of Lancelot (212). Lastly, in *The Knight with the Lion*, it is Gawain who urges Yvain to go on his fateful adventuring for knightly deeds, the journey on which he stays too long and loses his lady (326). Having identified the four main ideals of open communication, seeking experience in foreign lands, passionate devotion to something outside of oneself, and a middle path in serving both honor and love, I now turn to *The Story of the Grail*.

The Ideal in The Story of the Grail

Though unfinished, *The Story of the Grail* is Chrétien's longest romance. Its hero, Perceval, is quite unlike the previous heroes. Those heroes were either already knights (Erec, Lancelot, and Yvain) or would obviously become knights without difficulty (Alexander and Cligès), whereas Perceval starts the story completely naive. The romance also gives Gawain (who can reasonably be expected to be connected to the main ideal here as he was in the previous romances) a much larger role than he had in any previous romance. Before looking at Perceval and Gawain, I start with the prologue as a guide.

The prologue starts with the Parable of the Sower, a direct statement that Chrétien wants the story to produce a bounty (381). Indeed it has; because of its unfinished state, there has been no shortage of continuations and writing about it. If he had intended to finish it himself, however, perhaps he had something else in mind, and the rest of the prologue may tell us what it was. He contrasts vainglory and charity by declaring them to be opposites. He declares that Philip gives "gifts of charity; for he consults no one except his noble honest heart, which urges him to do good." Chrétien then states that this charity makes Philip "more worthy than Alexander." Lastly, Chrétien calls it "the greatest story that has ever been told in royal court" (382). Since it surpasses his earlier romances, perhaps its ideal surpasses them as well. We now have enough hints with which to analyze Perceval and Gawain.

Perceval starts out as a simpleton: knowing nothing of knighthood, when he sees knights for the first time, he thinks they are angels (382). Upon getting to speak to one, he immediately asks questions about all his equipment and how the knight got it, learning that the other man was knighted by Arthur (383–85). Thus he goes from believing that a knight is an angel to learning that he can actually become one of these "angels" in a very short time. The effect on him is profound, and he immediately sets off. Though he sees his mother faint from his departure, he continues on anyway (388–89). From these first few opening pages, it seems that this story is about knighthood itself, for that is what Perceval leaves home in quest for: to be a knight, whatever the cost. First, having not remembered his mother's parting advice properly, he meets a maiden in a tent, and forcibly kisses her and takes her ring (389–90). Although not explicitly stated, it seems likely that he felt his mother's advice was about how to be a good knight, and thus he was eager to follow it. Then he reaches Arthur's court. He receives no formal ceremony of knighthood, but Kay, ever with venomous tongue and on behalf of Arthur, "grants" Perceval the armor of the Red Knight, which he wanted more than anything when he first saw it (393). Before Perceval departs, Kay slaps a maiden for laughing and kicks the jester for a previous prophecy, which was: "This maiden will not laugh until she has seen the man who will be the supreme lord among all knights" (394). Perceval then departs to claim the armor, killing the Red Knight in the process (395).

Perceval does not return to Arthur. Instead, he rides on, and next comes to Gornemant. More than anyone else so far in the story, Perceval actually pays very close attention to everything he says and does, for he teaches Perceval the knightly ways of arms and armor (399–402). Perceval even says to him: "I truly want to know as much as you do about knighthood" — further proof that the story is still about Perceval's quest to be a knight (400). Here, Gornemant does formally bestow knighthood on Perceval, for he tells him so and attaches his spur and girds on his sword (401–02). He also gives Perceval the fateful advice to not talk too much. Upon leaving Gornemant, Perceval next comes to the castle of Blancheflor. As a new knight, he indeed proves his valor by defeating Anguingueron and Clamadeu each in single combat, liberating Blancheflor's castle, and winning her love (409, 414). Now he can marry her and rule her lands — a pinnacle of knightly accomplishment, as we have seen with Erec, Alexander, Cligès, and Yvain. It is only from concern over his mother's fate, however, that he leaves the castle to go find her (417). This is a manifestation of an incompleteness in him, despite his accomplishments, and it will indeed be seen that something is missing.

Before he can return home to his mother, he reaches the Grail Castle for lodgings one evening and sees the mysterious procession of the lance and grail (419–21). The narrative's repeated references to them make it clear that the questions of why the lance bleeds and who is served by the grail are important. Yet Perceval, who at the beginning of the romance was asking questions about everything, keeps silent here due to a flaw in his training by Gornemant — that fateful advice to not talk too much. This suggests a flaw in knighthood itself that needs correcting, since there was a flaw in the training. It cannot be that Gornemant is not a great knight, since (in *Erec and Enide*) Gornemant is ranked fourth of the Knights of the Round Table, after only Gawain, Erec, and Lancelot (58). Perceval thus leaves the castle without asking the essential questions. He next meets his cousin, who lays bare his deficiency in failing to ask the questions (425). The first thing she says to explain why this is a failing is that asking would have healed the king and brought much good — this is an interesting thing for a knight to do, since it is a stark contrast to the usual thing that knights do: fight and kill. She also informs him of his mother's death, and tells him that he was the cause of it.

Perceval, who is no longer trying to go home to his mother, next comes across the lady from the tent that he had met at the very beginning and the Haughty Knight is with her. Perceval defeats him, orders him to make right the harm he caused his lady and sends him to King Arthur (429). Next, when Perceval is meditating on three drops of blood that he sees in the snow, Kay disrupts and challenges him (434). This leads to Perceval breaking Kay's arm, thus avenging the maiden whom Kay slapped. Here in both of these things, Perceval is doing deeds of charity, and setting things right that were wrong or left undone. Then he has a joyous meeting with Gawain and Arthur's court, which is disrupted by the arrival of the Loathly Damsel. She repeats the reproach on Perceval that his cousin gave, emphasizing his failure to ask about both the lance and the grail (438). Then she tells the rest of the court about some opportunities for deeds of chivalry. Perceval, however, is not interested in those specific opportunities — he instead swears to shirk from no adventure and not sleep at the same place two nights "until he had learned who was served from the grail and had found the bleeding lance and been told the true reason why it bled" (439). The romance then continues with Gawain's adventures for a while.

When it comes back to Perceval to reveal that five years have passed, it emphasizes that he has forgotten God during that time, though he has had no lack of successful chivalric adventures (457). He is jarred from his forgetfulness when a group of penitents informs him that he is doing wrong by bearing arms on Good Friday. The group informs him that they have confessed their sins to a nearby holy hermit and received forgiveness (458). Perceval is remorseful and weeps, and they direct him to the hermit. Weeping again, he seeks absolution, and confesses to the hermit that he had forgotten God and failed to ask questions about the lance and grail (459). The hermit informs him that this was due to the sorrow he caused his mother, which killed her. The hermit then reveals that he is Perceval's uncle and tells him who is served by the grail — it is Perceval's other uncle (460). The grail is revealed to bear a host — spiritual nourishment. The context of the grail being such a mystery in this romance serves to emphasize the great importance of spiritual nourishment and that this is essential even for a knight like Perceval who has accomplished great deeds. Perceval earnestly desires penance for his sins, and his uncle imposes the penance, which has a heavy emphasis on religious observance. Perceval remains with his uncle until Easter Sunday and receives communion, and the romance does not return to him before its end (461). I now turn to Gawain's role before further comment on Perceval.

Gawain's first action in the romance is at the scene where Perceval is meditating on the drops of blood on the snow. After Sagremor and Kay have paid for disrupting him, Gawain recognizes that it was not right for them to have done so, and instead goes to see if Perceval may be brought back by peaceful means, and he succeeds (434–36). After the Loathly Damsel has departed, Gawain is accused by Guinganbresil of dishonorably killing his lord (439).

Gawain pledges to answer the charge in battle, and the story turns to him. Gawain sets off to do so, and comes to a tournament that he tries to avoid entering due to his commitment to answering the charge against him (443). He relents and enters the tournament, however, due to the earnest entreaties of a woman seeking his aid in defending her honor (447). He succeeds. He next goes to the castle of the man he was accused of killing, but after a brief adventure there, the reckoning between him and Guinganbresil is postponed for a year on the advice of a wise vavasour and Gawain is charged with finding and bringing back the bleeding lance (456). Gawain sets out for it, and the story turns back briefly to Perceval to recount his rediscovery of God on Good Friday.

Gawain next comes across a grieving maiden and a wounded knight. The knight warns him of a dangerous adventure ahead, and Gawain sets off for it (462). He meets the Haughty Damsel, who heaps endless abuse on him, preemptively condemns any kind of chivalrous behavior from him, and seemingly seeks to see him humiliated instead (463–65). Gawain reaches the Castle of Marvels, where he is told that to end its enchantments, there must come a knight who is "perfectly wise and generous, lacking all covetousness, fair and noble, bold and loyal, with no trace of wickedness or evil" (474). Gawain accepts the challenge, enters the castle, sits upon the Bed of Marvels and survives, thus breaking the enchantments and freeing its inhabitants (476–77). These include Arthur's mother, Gawain's mother, and Gawain's sister, although he doesn't know this at first, until he later crosses the Perilous Ford and meets Guiromelant who tells him (487–88). Guiromelant, it turns out, also has a grudge against Gawain and wants to challenge him to battle (489). Gawain returns across the Perilous Ford to the Haughty Damsel, who now treats him much more nicely and begs forgiveness for her wicked behavior (490). The romance then cuts off with Gawain orchestrating what would likely be a joyous family reunion with Arthur's court and that of the Castle of Marvels, where Gawain will also face Guiromelant in battle — or perhaps find a way to avert it (492–494).

What this all has to do with Perceval, the grail, or the lance is not immediately clear. One might accuse Chrétien here of turning into one of his continuators who has rambled on with no clear purpose and still not managed to finish the story. However, a theme emerges here with Gawain's actions: it is he who is a model of charity and of doing selfless deeds for others. He seeks a peaceful solution to getting Perceval to Arthur's court, enters the tournament to give aid to a woman, is courteous to the Haughty Damsel despite her abuse, liberates the Castle of Marvels, seeks to settle with Guiromelant without battle, and seeks to arrange a joyous family reunion. In all this, Gawain does not have a shred of vainglory; when asked if he is a Knight of the Round Table, he even says: "I wouldn't dare say that I'm one of the most esteemed" (480). Of Gawain, it can truly be said, like of Philip in the prologue, that "he consults no one except his noble honest heart, which urges him to do good" (381). Though some of Perceval's deeds show charity, they pale in comparison to Gawain's, and Perceval started the story with virtually no charity or concern for others whatsoever. Gawain is the model of charity that Perceval must emulate to truly be the great knight he desires to be. This is ultimately not Gawain's story, because the world of the romances is one where "heroes were in the process of realizing their destiny" (Baumgartner 217). Gawain, already being fully realized, stands outside of destiny, hence his presence as a counterpoint in all the romances, especially in this one.

Although unfinished, one can nevertheless see an ideal emerge from it. Perceval quested to be a knight, and became a great one — yet he quested further because something was missing, represented by not knowing whom the grail served. This missing element was revealed to be spiritual nourishment, served to a member of his own family — and it is his penitence and remorse that led to gaining this knowledge. Analogically, however, one can see this spiritual nourishment as serving the "family" of knighthood, for Perceval's family is indeed filled with knights, and that knighthood itself is incomplete without this spiritual element. Had the romance continued, I would have expected Perceval, having integrated this

299

spiritual element at last, to demonstrate the Gawain-like charity of a noble honest heart. Since it is charity that makes Philip greater than Alexander, Perceval would need much charity to ultimately be the "supreme lord among all knights," greater than even Gawain. So rather than communicating an ideal that is an aspect of knighthood, this romance communicates the ideal of aspiring to knighthood itself, and weaves into it the all-important values of spirituality and charity as the essential crown of knighthood, without which questing and adventuring will not avail, as with Perceval's five years of forgetting God.

Conclusion

Together, the romances sketch out how a knight may aspire to be a model of chivalry. The first four put the focus on his own actions and attitudes, but *The Story of the Grail* puts the focus on his need for spirituality, charity, and doing selfless deeds for others. It is the greatest of the romances because it seeks to improve knighthood by integrating this ideal into the desire for knighthood. To have such an influence on the order of knighthood itself, Chrétien would certainly desire his romance to be bountiful. Now may be answered the question: Whom does (the Story of) the Grail serve? It serves knighthood itself with spiritual nourishment to guide it toward its completion through the charity of a noble honest heart.

Works Cited

Baumgartner, Emmanuèle. "Chrétien's Medieval Influence: From the Grail Quest to the Joy of the Court." Trans. Véronique Zara. In *A Companion to Chrétien de Troyes*, eds. Norris J. Nancy and Joan Tasker Grimbert. Suffolk: D. S. Brewer, 2005. 214-27. Print.

Chrétien de Troyes. *Arthurian Romances*. Trans. William W. Kibler and Carleton W. Carroll. London: Penguin Books, 1991. Print.

Cligès = Chrétien de Troyes. *Arthurian Romances*.

Erec and Enide = Chrétien de Troyes. *Arthurian Romances*.

Keen, Maurice. *Chivalry*. New Haven: Yale UP, 1984. Print.

Knight of the Cart = Chrétien de Troyes. *Arthurian Romances.*

Knight with the Lion = Chrétien de Troyes. *Arthurian Romances.*

Pickens, Rupert T. "*Le Conte du Graal*: Chrétien's Unfinished Last Romance." In *A Companion to Chrétien de Troyes*, eds. Norris J. Nancy and Joan Tasker Grimbert. Suffolk: D. S. Brewer, 2005. 169-87. Print.

Story of the Grail = Chrétien de Troyes. *Arthurian Romances.*

Zink, Michel. *Medieval French Literature: An Introduction*. Trans. Jeff Rider. Binghamton: Center for Medieval and Early Renaissance Studies, 1995. Print.

Afterword

Postface

I think that it is only when one becomes a Skald that one can truly taste the Mead of Poetry in its greatest glory. Another has said that it is only when one becomes a Master that real Rune-Work begins. Under a different initiatory system, it may equally well be said that it is only when one becomes a Knight that one's true Grail Quest begins.

This is my esoteric journey so far. However, it is not the end of my journey. It is only the end of the beginning. What comes next for me? The Skald must make and pour his Mead. The Rune-Master must galdor and teach. The Knight must defend Tradition and quest for the Holy Grail. What comes next for you? Another step on your own great quest — if you dare.

Benediction

> Heartened and hale be all
> who heed this strongest Mead:
> quest for your seed inside
> of Self to fly through sky.
> A world awaits of sights
> — a wondrous brilliant thrill —
> reached by the runes here vouched
> through road so full of wode!

ᛒᚨ·ᚹᛁᛚᛚ·ᛁ·ᚨᚠᛏ·ᚦᚨᛏ·ᚠᚨᚱᛚᛗᚾ·ᛁᛏ·ᛒᛗ